NLP AT WORK

The new business agenda of the '90s focuses on working with change and developing people's potential and performance. The *People Skills for Professionals* series brings this leading theme to life with a range of practical human resource guides for anyone who wants to get the best from their people in the world of the learning organization.

Other Titles in the Series

COACHING FOR PERFORMANCE
The New Edition of the Practical Guide
John Whitmore

CONSTRUCTIVE CONFLICT MANAGEMENT
Managing to Make a Difference
John Crawley

EMPOWERED!
A Practical Guide to Leadership in the
Liberated Organisation
Rob Brown and Margaret Brown

LEADING YOUR TEAM
How to Involve and Inspire Teams
Andrew Leigh and Michael Maynard

LEARNING TO LEAD
A Workbook On Becoming A Leader
Warren Bennis and Joan Goldsmith

MANAGING TRANSITIONS
Making the Most of Change
William Bridges

POSITIVE MANAGEMENT
Assertiveness for Managers
Paddy O'Brien

THE POWER OF INFLUENCE
Intensive Influencing Skills at Work
Tom E. Lambert

THE STRESS WORK BOOK
Revised edition
Eve Warren and Caroline Toll

THE TRUST EFFECT
Creating the High Trust, High Performance
Organization
Larry Reynolds

NLP AT WORK

The difference that makes a difference in business

Sue Knight

NICHOLAS BREALEY
PUBLISHING

LONDON

To Colin ('Spence') for your inspiration, creative support and trust.

I wrote this book my friends and associates as a way of saying thank you and I wrote it especially for my sons James and Alex.

First published by
Nicholas Brealey Publishing in 1995

Reprinted 1995 (twice, with corrections), 1996 (three times), 1997 (twice), 1998

36 John Street
London
WC1N 2AT
Tel: +44 (0) 171 430 0224
Fax: +44 (0) 171 404 8311

671 Clover Drive
Santa Rosa
CA 95401, USA
Tel: (707) 566 8006
Fax: (707) 566 8005

ISBN 1-85788-070-6

British Library Cataloguing in Publication Data
A catalogue record for this book is available
from the British Library.

Illustrations by Mike Davison and Colin Spencer

Printed and bound in Finland by Werner Söderström Oy

Contents

Acknowledgements

There are many people I wish to thank for their help and influence in writing this book. In particular:

John Grinder and Richard Bandler for the ideas and thinking that inspire and influence so many people in the world today.

Gene Early, my earliest and most influential teacher of NLP, who continues to demonstrate with awesome congruence the sheer elegance of NLP in action.

David Gordon who brought fun and energy to the UKTC training programmes (the first NLP training school in this country) where I first studied NLP.

Robert Dilts for his inspiring demonstrations that left me knowing how much I had to learn, and for his genius and creativity in his developments of NLP.

Pat, Caroline, Alison, Ellen and Jus, my administrators, for their patience and time in typing and editing the text.

Monica Hayes, Peter Naylor and Kevin Daffey for their expert scrutiny and advice on my script.

Lorraine Calland, Ian Ross, Lesley Gosling and Marie Faire for their support, friendship, expertise and inspiration in the development and application of NLP to business.

Ken and Kate Back for our long and fruitful association through their assertiveness training programmes.

Nick Brealey for his guidance and trust throughout the process of writing this book.

Puy des Vignes where I found the space and the peace to write and rewrite!

The NLP stories have now become a part of the folklore and it has become difficult to trace the sources. Some of the stories I have used are my own. 'The beast in the valley' was written by Joy Scholes, a delegate on one of our courses. I suspect that the source of many more was David Gordon. I especially wish to thank John Fowles for his permission to use 'The prince and the magician' from *The Magus*. Thank you to all the story authors. The stories made NLP learning fun, intriguing and enlightening. I hope the stories I have used in this book will do the same for you.

Sue Knight Associates

Sue Knight Associates provide tailor-made in-company consultancy and training, one to one high performance coaching, and a series of NLP open courses, conferences and seminars. Sue Knight is also available for international speaking engagements.

Sue Knight Associates can be contacted at:

PO Box 1008, Slough, SL1 8DB
By phone on 01628 667868
By fax on 01628 667865
By e-mail on pat@synectic.demon.co.uk

What is NLP?

Neuro Linguistic Programming (NLP) is the study of what works in thinking, language and behaviour. It is a way of coding and reproducing excellence that enables you consistently to achieve the results that you want both for yourself and your business.

The business world is changing so rapidly that the need for expertise in specialist skills has been replaced by the need to learn and differentiate. More and more organisations are seeking to create a **learning organisation**: one in which the individuals manage their own development and learn to unleash their capabilities, and work to their peak potential. However, this cannot be achieved by using methods from the past. Do what you have always done and you get what you have always got! The key to the future lies within individuals. It is their ability to manage their thinking, their conflicts and their experience that will ultimately make the difference between those individuals and organisations that will lead the way into a new, exciting, creative and cooperative future, and those that will rapidly fall by the wayside as they attempt to follow.

Many of the current books about the future of the business world suggest that companies need to undergo a major **reengineering**. However, the secret to the success of this reengineering lies not in revamping the structure of the whole organisation, but in reprogramming your thinking and attitude

The key to future success

Change from within

from within. The culture of an organisation is an expression of the people within it, especially those at the top. The patterns of a leader inevitably become the patterns of the organisation of which he or she is a part. Whether or not you are a manager in name or job title, you too are a leader. You influence the environment of which you are a part. By understanding and influencing your own internal patterns you influence your experience. Success comes from within. Your success depends on your ability to achieve an exquisite level of excellence in everything that you think, say and do. Peter Senge introduces the concept of personal mastery in his book *The Fifth Discipline*. NLP provides the 'how' to achieve this.

Excellence is context specific

By learning to master the techniques and thinking in this book you will begin to achieve more of what you really want. More than that, you will learn how to reproduce excellence in any skill that you choose. Excellence is context specific. Many teaching models fail because they assume that what works in one context will work in another. What makes an inspiring leader in one company may be quite different to what works in another. NLP enables you to code excellence and to enhance it so that you can establish what really works for you in your unique environment.

More specifically, NLP can enable you to:

- accelerate your ability to learn so that you can not only manage change but initiate it, enabling you to lead the way in your particular interests and field of work;

- set compelling outcomes for yourself, ones that by their very nature take on a momentum of their own and maximise the chances that you will achieve what you want, both for yourself personally and for your business;

- build high quality relationships with the people around you and those with whom you come into contact in your everyday work and life;

- heighten your sensitivity to yourself and others, so that you are aware of subtle shifts in behaviour and attitude and of the effects of the way you communicate;

- develop your flexibility so that you have more choices and consequently more influence over the situations in your life;

- improve your ability to generate commitment, cooperation and enthusiasm in the people around you;

- manage your thoughts and feelings so that you are in control of your emotions and your destiny;

- develop your ability to tap into your unconscious mind and draw on its superior power and potential.

The skills and thinking outlined above, and many more that NLP offers you, can transform your experience in all kinds of situations. In business especially, NLP is the difference that makes the difference in communication, motivation, influence, negotiation, leadership, empowerment, self-development, goal setting, organisational development... the list is endless. You will find your own applications — that is the real joy of NLP.

The difference that makes the difference

HOW DOES NLP WORK?

NLP is the study of exceptional talent. It is the study of both the conscious and the unconscious processes that combine to enable people to do what they do. NLP pays very little attention to what people say they do, as that usually bears very little or no resemblance to what they *actually* do. You might think that by asking top achievers how they succeed you would get precise answers. You would be wrong! The key to success is often unknown at the conscious level. The previously unknown pieces are sometimes referred to as the magic of NLP. It is not magic, just an awareness of what really makes the difference that is so often missing in more traditional models and techniques. Using the tools of NLP you can elicit these unknown pieces so that you can 'code' talent. That is the secret of the magic of NLP.

There will be things that *you* do that you do not (yet) understand. Do you know, for example:

The magic of NLP

- what you do that is different in those relationships where you have exquisite rapport — where you know what the other person is going to say before they say it?

- how you control your feelings in some situations when in others you lose control?

● in those situations where you feel especially confident, how you generate that inner feeling of calm and certainty even when everything else is stacked against you?

In short, when you know the answers to these questions and others like them, you begin to have more choice over the way you think, feel and behave. You have more influence over your own destiny.

THE NAME

NLP stands for Neuro Linguistic Programming.

Neuro   refers to your neurological system, the way you use your senses of sight, hearing, touch, taste and smell to translate your experience into thought processes, both conscious and unconscious. It relates to your physiology as well as your mind and how these function as one system. Much of NLP is about increasing your awareness of your neurological system and learning to manage it.

Linguistic   refers to the way you use language to make sense of your experience and how you communicate that experience to yourself and others. Your language patterns are an expression of who you are and how you think.

Programming   is the coding of experience. A program is a series of steps designed to achieve a specific result. The results you achieve and the effects you create in yourself and others are the consequence of your personal programs. There is a sequence of behaviour and thinking patterns that results in your experience. Through awareness of these sequences you can code the structure of your own and other people's experience.

Some say that John Grinder and Richard Bandler, the founders of NLP, shut themselves away in a log cabin in the Californian mountains and asked themselves the question, 'What shall we call this work?' John Grinder is a linguist, Richard Bandler was at that time a programmer and a mathematician. They had been studying the way the mind works. Consequently they came up with the name Neuro Linguistic Programming, an integration of all these elements.

Much of NLP is not new. Many of the ideas had been around for years before John and Richard brought them together under the heading of NLP. They used their understanding about the sequence of thinking and language patterns to code excellence. They gave a new purpose to this body of knowledge, and in the process of coding excellence they made their own discoveries. NLP was born and continues to grow.

I worked as a management consultant and trainer for several years before I discovered NLP. For years I taught subjects such as objective setting, motivation, leadership, influencing and communication skills. And for years I struggled with the problem of really making a difference for those managers and trainers that I taught. Yet I still could not fathom out why much of this teaching faded. These same delegates, no matter how enthusiastic and committed they were, quickly returned to their original ways of thinking and behaving. The simplicity and elegance of NLP is that it is about what works. It sounds so obvious, yet part of the magic lies in discovering precisely what does work. In the years I have been teaching and using NLP, I have witnessed more powerful sustainable change than ever before. By mastering the approaches covered in this book, you can learn to make the changes that you *really* want and that fit with the people that you want to have around you.

The changes you really want

THE JARGON

With a name like Neuro Linguistic Programming you won't be surprised to learn that NLP is packed with jargon. Representational systems, submodalities, metaprograms, presuppositions, perceptual positions! And the meta model, a model about language, includes even more — universal quantifiers, modal operators of necessity, complex equivalence ...

I have chosen to avoid jargon wherever possible, since my aim in writing this book is to provide a simple and usable guide to NLP at work.

THE PRINCIPLES OF NLP

NLP has evolved a culture of its own. This culture includes principles concerning the way NLP is taught and used. These are the following:

NLP starts with you

- NLP starts with yourself. It is only by learning how to manage yourself that you can then influence others. By understanding how the techniques and thinking work for you, you will be better able to facilitate change in the environment of which you are a part.

- The unconscious mind is considerably more powerful than the conscious mind. NLP employs techniques that teach to both the conscious and the unconscious. NLP training at its best will incorporate many of the elements that are characteristic of accelerated learning and are therefore powerful and fast.

- Congruence in what you are, what you believe, what you say and do is the recipe for personal success. You can expect to feel confident in the presence of a skilled NLP practitioner that the signals they give out are a true representation of who they are and what they believe.

Code of conduct

NLP is a way of thinking and behaving. It can become a code of conduct. I have no doubt that NLP applied with elegance and respect can enhance the quality of everything you do.

NLP is based on the premise that you already have within you all the resources that you will ever need and it therefore concentrates on drawing out these capabilities and skills. Learning NLP is a process of growth and personal development.

THE HISTORY OF NLP

Richard Bandler and John Grinder began by choosing to study people they considered to be excellent, particularly in the areas of communication and the management of change. They studied:

- therapists, such as Fritz Perls, Virginia Satir and Milton Erickson, and discovered how they used positive association, metaphors and ways of building rapport through behaviour and language;

- the work of linguists Alfred Korzybski and Noam Chomsky, through which they developed their learning about presuppositions and language patterns;

- many others including the anthropologist Gregory Bateson and the psychoanalyst Paul Watzlawick.

These original findings provided techniques that allowed the study of NLP to grow. By using the rapport-building skills Bandler and Grinder were able to create an atmosphere of ease and openness with other 'figures of excellence' that accelerated their ability to continue their studies. By understanding how their own language patterns represented the patterns in their thinking, they were able to make different choices about how they proceeded with their work. And so it continues. NLP is a generative process.

You might wonder what connection all these people have with the business world. How can the work of therapists and anthropologists have relevance to our continually changing, high-tech environment? The clue is in the 'changing'. All these early models were concerned with change. Fritz Perls, Virginia Satir and Milton Erickson were masters of change. The processes they used have absolute parallels in the change that we seek to manage in business for individuals and organisations alike.

NLP work today benefits from all that has gone before. The techniques we learn are techniques which we use as we continue to learn. It is a process of continuous improvement. One of my delegates once said to me, 'What do I do when there is no more NLP learning to do?' I believe that that day need never come as we move along this road of discovery.

Continuous improvement

COMING TOGETHER

I studied and experienced NLP training for more than a year before the pieces started to fall into place. I could use bits of it but I didn't really have a sense of the whole. And then one day in the heart of Cumbria...

I could feel the dampness of my palms as the engineers walked into the training room. The last batch, 18 of them. These were the ones who had avoided all the previous meetings. The company had decided to mop up the stragglers in one bunch. Normally there would only be 12 in a group. Several of them were having to forfeit their day in lieu to be here. 'Here' was a dark, cool training room. Outside it was bright and sunny. No one spoke to me as they entered the room unless I spoke to them, and even then they kept the response as brief as possible. They sat, arms and legs crossed, with a 'so what do you think you're going to teach us?' look on their faces, or so it seemed to me. I had a sick, sinking feeling in the pit of my stomach. I was facing three days and evenings with them. I began the standard introductory questions: 'What do you want from this training?' The spokesman for the group answered, 'Quite frankly, love, we don't want to be here at all. If I weren't here I would be on my allotment digging potatoes and I've no doubt about where I'd choose to be.'

For several years I had worked with a colleague, Charles, with many other groups from this company. Charles' reputation with these engineers was unsurpassed. They liked and admired him. At that moment I chose to be Charles. I adopted the sort of posture he would adopt. Charles typically sat fairly quietly at the beginning of this sort of session, and made no attempt to impress. I did the same. He always stressed that everyone deserved respect and that each person had a wealth of experience to offer. I imagined what it would be like to believe that about this group. Metaphors played a large part in the way Charles made a point. Often the metaphors with groups like this were to do with sport, snooker especially. Fortunately I had picked up a few tips along the way, so this was an option for me too. I took on more and more of what I knew to be Charles' style, thinking, beliefs and values. I began to feel more comfortable and confident. Slowly some of the group members uncrossed their arms and began to sit forward. A few even asked questions. Things continued to improve throughout that first day. My real indicator of success was when the spokesman came up to me at the end of the second day and said, 'You're OK.' He had hardly said anything until that moment. I responded the way Charles would, with a knowing smile. It was a success. I was invited to do many more of these sessions with groups in other divisions. This in a simple form was NLP in action.

PART I

THE ELEMENTS

OF NLP

A journey of discovery

NLP brings together many techniques that have been around for years, and combines them with discoveries that are new. It is both a study of masters of change, some of whom are no longer alive, and a recognition of the talents that exist within each person. NLP is a journey of discovery. When I decided to write this book my publisher and I discussed in detail what would be an appropriate structure. NLP didn't evolve in a neat chronological sequence — it sort of exploded into the world of therapy and now it is doing the same in the world of business. So how could I structure the subject in a way that enables you quickly to grasp the elements and begin to appreciate and experience the power of the whole? I experimented with many approaches before we decided to use the name Neuro Linguistic Programming as the basis for the structure. Easier said than done!

The elements of NLP don't fit perfectly into the categories of Neuro, Linguistic and Programming. Nevertheless these headings act as useful umbrellas under which to introduce the subject. I ask for the tolerance of the purists among you who could argue about the exact categorisation of each of the elements. Equally, I emphasise that the content of the book is by no means complete in its coverage of NLP. I have chosen those pieces of NLP that I believe serve as a useful introduction and are most relevant to work.

The first 'technique umbrella' is **Neuro**. Neuro is concerned with the way you use your mind, your body and your senses to think and to make sense of your experience. The more awareness you have of your thinking patterns, the more flexibility and therefore the more influence you have over your destiny.

Thinking power

I start this section with **thinking patterns**. The discovery of the unique ways we think opened the doors to many of the models for change which are covered in Part 2. You can read many books that will encourage you to 'think positively', to 'stay calm', to 'keep control'. NLP offers the 'how' to do this, and this section in particular will help you to expand your thinking power. NLP does this, not by prescribing fixed techniques that work for some, but by enabling you to explore what it is that you do when you 'think positively', 'stay calm' and 'keep control', for example. You have your own unique ways of accessing and using these kinds of resources, no matter how infrequently or how briefly you may have used them in the past. Once you understand the elements of your personal 'program' you can run that program when you choose. This section will raise your awareness of how you do what you do — a stepping stone to personal mastery.

Also within the Neuro section I include **filters**. Your perception of situations and people is governed by the filters through which you experience the world. By recognising these filters you can increase your understanding of your ability to relate to the unique styles of the people around you. For example, have you ever noticed how in meetings some people talk about what is missing and different about ideas and proposals, whereas others search for what they like and how these ideas compare to other similar ones. Unfortunately, together they seem to be talking different languages. All too often the people who search for what is missing and different are labelled as 'difficult'.

Unique styles

Under the heading of **Linguistics**, I include **language patterns**, **precision questions** and **metaphor**. The ways of using language to facilitate change formed a large part of the early work of John Grinder and Richard Bandler. In business, language is one of the most readily available forms of influence. The section on language patterns explores how you can use each of your senses to enrich your language and bring it alive. With precision questions you can learn how to generate quality information, the lifeblood of business. Precision questions are also undoubtedly one of the most powerful tools for challenging the constraints that people create for themselves. The use of these questions provides the solution to the challenge of empowerment. Whereas precision questions work largely at the conscious level, metaphor is a way of utilising the unconscious mind in the process of change. Learn how to recognise and use metaphors to engage your listeners' minds and elegantly bypass conscious resistance.

Quality information

And finally, the **Programming** part of NLP — **modelling**. In modelling you learn not only how to bring together all the skills of NLP to elicit and code exceptional talent, but also how to access the hidden resources within yourself so that you can begin to realise your true potential.

These elements can be used in different ways. As independent techniques they will enable you to improve the quality of your relationships and gain greater control and choice over the way you live your life and the results you achieve. Additionally, even though many of these elements were discovered through the process of coding excellence, they are now also used to enhance the quality of the coding process itself. For example, your awareness and understanding of the finer distinctions in language and behaviour will enable you to discover the difference that makes the difference in the models of excellence that you choose to study.

You may come across people with different views and thinking as to what constitute the elements of NLP. That is fine. I believe it is important that we each take NLP for what it is, a process of discovery. The elements I have included here are an introduction to NLP. Not only are there more already known and taught, but undoubtedly more are being discovered as I write. I offer you these core skills as a way of developing your awareness and sensitivity both to yourself and to others. If you achieve that, then you will already have begun the process of change.

Neuro

Many of the traditional models of change and influence have
sought to bring about change through manipulation of other
people and the environment. The reality is that you cannot
change other people, you can only change yourself. Your
environment is tempered by the mental thought patterns that
you hold.

There are some people, for example, who only see good in
others. They have no representation for bad. In their world bad
doesn't exist.

Your thoughts leak out in everything that you do, often in
ways that are outside your conscious awareness. However, in
so doing, these thoughts send out signals to the world about
what you want, what you believe and who you are. And the
world responds to these signals. Consequently the key to
influencing these responses is to change the inner signals. NLP
offers you the opportunity to manage these inner
representations and signals. You begin to tap into the potential
of the world's most powerful computer — your mind.

Your thoughts send out signals

By learning how to manage your thoughts you can:

- change your experience of situations and people;

- influence the reactions you get;

- hold memories in a way that supports the person you
  want to be;

- create the future you want;

- build the relationships you would like.

And this is only the starter list. You can learn to manage your mind in such a way that it works for you in any way you want.

Thinking Patterns *1.1*

Thinking patterns and the ability to manage them are a large part of what makes the difference with NLP. It can take time to learn how to exercise all the different components. However, each development in your skill to do this will lead to increased mastery over your own experience. This skill, combined with other NLP skills and techniques, gives you the ability to reproduce not only other people's experience but also your own. Your increased awareness of how you do what you do leads automatically to increased choices for you.

Your brain is an unknown and largely untapped resource. The connections you make and the way you represent memories, ideas and information are unique to you. When you understand the nature of these representations, you begin to have control of your mind and consequently of your experience. What you think is what you are.

You take in information through each of the senses of sight, hearing, touch, taste and smell. You represent this information in your mind as a combination of these sensory systems. Your thinking patterns are a part of how you 'code' your experience. NLP gives you the ability to influence from within. By learning to manage your thoughts you learn how to create the life and career you want for yourself. Life is literally what you make it.

Unique thought patterns

PREFERENCES IN THINKING PATTERNS

Let's explore some of these differences in thinking patterns.

Think of 'coffee'. What comes to mind?

Does a picture come to mind? Maybe you imagined coffee cups and a coffee pot.

Or maybe you heard the sound of coffee percolating. Or maybe the noise as it was poured into the cup.

Then again maybe it was more of a feeling. The feel of the coffee cup, the taste of the coffee or the aroma of the coffee as it is brewing.

Maybe it was a combination of some or all of these different ways of thinking.

These different ways of thinking are:

Pictures, sounds and feelings

Visual   You think in pictures. You represent ideas, memory and imagination as mental images.

Auditory   You think in sounds. These sounds could be voices or noises, e.g. the sound of coffee percolating.

Feelings   You represent thoughts as feelings which might be internal emotion or the thought of a physical touch. We can include taste and smell in this category of feelings.

You will find that you probably have a preference for one system over the others, both in the way you think and in the way you communicate.

   Is it any surprise that 'communication' is one of the most widely recognised problems in business today? Consider the business meeting and the level of frustration that so many people express with the meetings they attend. Even in meetings where an objective is agreed, it is likely that each member of the meeting will represent a successful conclusion in a different way. For example, some of the various ways that members of a meeting might imagine a successful outcome could include:

Business meetings

Visual   An image of all the agreed actions written up on a whiteboard with names against each one.

Auditory   People talking to each other at the close of the meeting making comments such as, 'That's been really useful. I know exactly what my department has to do next.'

Feelings   Thoughts about shaking hands with other members of the meeting and a soft, warm feeling inside.

Once you become aware of these differences you can begin to take account of them. Part 2 deals with how to use these core skills to good effect in business.

You may already recognise preferences in your thinking. To check this out you can use the questionnaire in Chapter 3.1 of the Toolkit — Identify Your Preferred Thinking Pattern.

EYE MOVEMENTS

A clue to the way you think is given in the way you move your eyes. For example, is there someone close to you now who considers themselves to be a good speller? Ask them to spell 'phenomenon'. Watch their eyes as they do so. If they are really skilled ask them to spell 'phenomenon' backwards. Good spellers will typically look up, eyes right or eyes left, to see the word in their mind's eye. Because they can see it written out they have no difficulty in spelling it backwards. It is as if it is there on the page in front of them.

Did your school teacher ever say to you, 'You won't find the answer on the ceiling'? The truth of it is you probably would! Your eyes are an indication of how you are thinking.

The usual way in which these eye movements are organised is as follows:

up and right (their right)
for constructed, imagined images
e.g. you floating on air or you with blue hair (assuming you haven't got or had blue hair!)

up and left
for remembered images
e.g. the scenes on your holidays, the image of your school

sideways right
for constructed sounds
e.g. your boss talking to you in a Donald Duck voice, the sound of a cat barking

sideways left
for remembered sounds
e.g. your favourite piece of music, the sound of a bath running

down and right
for feelings and internal emotions
e.g. the touch of silk, the feelings of confidence or sadness

down and left
for internal dialogue
e.g. what you say to yourself before you give an important presentation, or what you say to yourself before you go to sleep at night

straight ahead, defocused
for visual images, remembered or created
e.g. the faces of your close friends, the way you imagine the route might look on a journey you are about to take

These are the usual eye movements for right-handed people, but there are exceptions. Left-handed people may have some of the positions reversed. It is important to check. It is usual to have variations only in reversal of sides. **Visual** is always up (or straight ahead). **Auditory** is always sideways (looking towards the ears), and **feelings** and inner dialogues are always down.

And if you think about it, expressions in language support this concept. We talk about:

- 'things looking up'

- 'chin up' — to get out of 'feeling down'

- 'downright angry'

Time to think

Developing your awareness of other people's eye movements will help you to develop your sensitivity to their thinking and their emotions. If you ask someone a question and they look away to access the information they need for the answer, then there is no point in saying anything else until they have finished their mental processing. When they have finished they will typically make eye contact with you again.

I have heard some people say they become irritated when the person with whom they are having a conversation won't make constant eye contact with them. To do this for most people would be to stop thinking!

Understanding these distinctions in thinking begins to give you an insight into the way you and others access and process information. Later in the book you will learn how to use this understanding to help build rapport, improve understanding and influence and to code excellence.

FINER DISTINCTIONS IN THINKING

Within each of the main thinking patterns of visual, auditory and feelings there are finer distinctions. For example, the colour and clarity of an image, the tone and volume of a sound, the strength and location of a feeling. People who have control over their emotions and their experience have the ability to manipulate these fine distinctions in their thinking. Learning to exercise and extend your range of thinking patterns leads to mental agility in your ability to think in the way you want, just as physical exercise leads to bodily flexibility.

You return home and walk into the kitchen area. The working surfaces are clean and white. On one surface is a blue ceramic bowl filled with fruit, vivid green apples, purple grapes and several bright yellow lemons. You pick up one of the lemons and feel the textured surface with your fingertips. You raise it to your nose and smell the sharp aroma. Also on the surface is a sharp kitchen knife and a wooden chopping board. You place the lemon on the board and slice through the middle of it. A fine mist of lemon juice sprays into the air. You pick up one half of the lemon and see the defined segments and pips, some of them cut through now. You raise this half to your mouth; the sharp aroma is even stronger now. You sink your teeth into the skin.

At this point the saliva flow in your mouth will probably have increased. This is the power of your thought process. The way you think affects your internal state which in turn triggers off a physical reaction, in this case the saliva flow. Your mind cannot distinguish between what is imagined and what is real.

Body and mind are one

For example:

Jim often had to give presentations as part of his work. Although he felt comfortable in one-to-one meetings, whenever he had to present to larger groups of half a dozen or more he felt uncomfortable and nervous. It was worse if he knew about the presentation several days in advance because he would start to imagine what could go wrong. In particular he would imagine a dark room, and although there were people in his image of the room their faces would be a blur. He would typically start telling himself in a harsh, critical internal voice the problems he might have. For example, he wouldn't be able to explain his points clearly, he would lose his place in his notes, people would get bored. If he heard himself speaking it would be in almost a whisper. He could see people straining forward to hear, or sitting back and looking away. He would feel a heavy, sick feeling in his stomach, his heart began to beat faster and his mouth felt dry. Beads of perspiration would break out on his forehead and hands.

And all this even before he gives the presentation!

The result is that you effectively 'dry run' your life in your own mind to the extent that you influence the eventual result. Your life becomes a self-fulfilling prophecy! You are what you think.

MANAGE YOUR THINKING PROCESS

Think about something you did last week. Now think of something you could have done last week but didn't. The question is, how do you know you did one and not the other? After all, these are only memories — one remembered, one created. How often have you had that experience of not knowing for sure whether you did something or not? 'Did I lock the front door?' 'Did I turn off the water heater?'

Past, present or future?

Think of something you did yesterday that you will do in an identical way tomorrow. It might be getting out of bed, or brushing your teeth or setting the alarm. How do you distinguish between the one you did yesterday and the one you will do tomorrow? *Can* you distinguish between what you did yesterday and what you will do tomorrow?

Many people distinguish between the past and the future according to where they position the images in their mind. For example, the past might be behind you or to your left. The future for some people is in front of them or to their right. Where is your past? Where is your future? And where is the present?

Identify two people that you know, one that you like and admire and one that you dislike. Now take the one you like and admire. In your thinking about this person:

- Do you see him or her, and if so, what is the quality of the image? For example is it bright or hazy, colour or black and white, moving or still?

- Are there any sounds associated with the thinking?

- What are the qualities of the sounds? Are they loud or faint, harsh or soft?

- What is the location of the sound?

- And what of the feelings? What do you experience exactly and where?

Now think of the person you dislike, and consider the same questions. What is similar in the quality of your thinking about the two and what is different? The content is irrelevant. It is the nature of your thinking that makes the difference.

This ability to distinguish between the various aspects of your own and other people's experience is the way you can determine the difference that makes the difference.

Let's consider these distinctions in thinking patterns in more detail.

Brightness	Bright or dim? Dull or sparkly?	*Visual distinctions*
Clarity	Dim and hazy or sharp and in focus?	
Size	Larger than life, life size or smaller than life?	
Colour/black and white	Full colour, shades of grey, partial colour, black and white?	
Location	In front of you, to one side, behind you?	
Distance	Close to or distant?	
Motion	Still snapshots or movies?	
Speed	Fast/slow?	
Framed/panoramic	Enclosed in a frame or panoramic?	
Sequence	In order/random/simultaneous images?	
Associated/dissociated	Are you seeing as if out of your own eyes (associated) or can you see yourself in the picture (dissociated)?	

Now take a few simple images and experiment with them.

Think, for example, of your journey to work. You can change your experience of this journey to make it better or worse by experimenting with your thinking about it. Start by changing some of the visual distinctions. For example, if it is dim turn up the brightness. Then put it back as it was. If it is still make it into a movie. Each time you experiment with a distinction return it to its original form before you experiment with another. This way you will be able to establish how a change in a specific distinction affects your experience of the situation, in this case the journey. You may find that your thinking about the journey becomes more relaxed, more stressful, more interesting or maybe more exciting.

You may find initially that you are not aware of any pictures in your thinking. This is not unusual. If this is the case, do the exercise with your eyes closed and allow yourself to become aware of what you do notice.

Auditory distinctions

Volume	How loud/quiet?
Speed	Fast or slow?
Location	Where is the source of the sound? Is it in front of you, to one side, behind you?
Distance	Is the sound close or far away?
Voice/sound	Is it a voice or can you hear other sounds? If it is a voice, whose voice is it and what tone is it in?
Pitch	High/low/mid range?
Continuous	Is the sound continuous or intermittent?

Take another memory, for example your last disagreement at work.

Experiment again, this time with the auditory distinctions. For example, if you can recall voices make them soft and whispery. Now give them a different accent. Make them loud and boomy, remembering to return the memory to its original state before experimenting with the next distinction.

Note how this experiment affects the quality of the memory. What starts as an unpleasant memory can become an amusing one just by changing the nature of the voices. Give someone the voice of a cartoon character, e.g. Bugs Bunny. What effect does that have?

Pressure	What sort of pressure can you feel? Is there a sense of being pushed, a general or specific pressure?	*Feelings distinctions*
Location	Where in your body do you experience any sensations?	
Motion	Is there movement to the feeling? Is it fluttery, steady, intermittent, tingling?	
Temperature	Hot/cold/damp?	
Intensity	Strong/weak?	
Pace	Is it a fast feeling/a slow one?	

Now think of a time when you felt joy. What does joy feel like to you and where exactly in your body do you experience it? Experiment again. This time experiment with the intensity of the feeling. Can you turn it up and down? Return the feeling to its original state. Change the pace of the feeling. Continue to experiment with each element of the feeling, returning it to its original state before you experiment with the next one.

You will find that in each case there will be one or two key distinctions for you. By changing these distinctions you can change the quality of your experience.

Jim experimented with his thinking about presentations, comparing it to his thinking about one-to-one meetings in which he did feel confident and relaxed. He discovered that the key distinctions for him were brightness, focus and the tone of voice with which he spoke to himself. By bringing the quality of his thinking about presentations into line with his thinking about one-to-one meetings, by making the image bright and in focus and by softening his internal voice tone, he noticed that he felt a steady rippling feeling in his chest. This was the same feeling he experienced in one-to-one meetings. This, for him, was the feeling that he associated with confidence.

There are some general trends in the distinctions associated with feelings of confidence, happiness and certainty. Not surprisingly there are expressions in everyday language that reflect this. For example:

● 'the future is looking brighter' as opposed to 'the future looks black';

● 'that's becoming clearer' as opposed to 'that's unclear'.

The richness of your internal thinking leaks through into your

Reprogramming your experience

SUMMARY

communication and into your experience. Enrich your thinking — enrich your life.

Once you have experienced something it becomes a memory. When you react to a memory you are reacting to the way you store that memory in your mind. Managing the distinctions in your thinking gives you the ability to influence and change the nature of your memories, so that you can store them in a way that results in you feeling the way you want to feel.

You can be sure that you already use distinctions in your thinking patterns in this way. Whenever you change your experience of something you are almost certain to have 'reprogrammed' the way you think about it. You may not have realised that this was what you were doing — but it was!

Many people become skilled at storing memories in a way that leads to depression or anger or other negative feelings. Why choose these when you could choose pleasure or peace? The same is true for the future. Why make yourself worried or frustrated about an event that hasn't occurred when you could be making yourself confident and comfortable? You might choose to keep some of the worry in the form of concern. The point is that you choose the state you want rather than it choosing you.

THOUGHT PROVOKERS

1   What sort of jobs do you think would best suit people whose thinking preference is:
    a. visual?   b. auditory?   c. feelings?

2   Think of a successful outcome of a regular meeting that you hold/attend. How do you think about this? Is it a picture? Do you hear sounds or conversation? Do you experience certain feelings?

3   In a social conversation with one of your colleagues, pay attention to their eye movements. Which eye movements do they use predominantly?

4   Think of a part of your work that you really enjoy. Now think of a part that you enjoy less well. How do the distinctions in your thinking vary?

5   Think of someone with whom you have a really good relationship. Now think of someone you find difficult to deal with. Compare the differences in your thinking about each person. What are the main distinctions?

One day a traveller was walking along a road on his journey from one village to another. As he walked he noticed a monk tilling the ground in the fields beside the road. The monk said 'Good day' to the traveller and the traveller nodded to the monk. The traveller then turned to the monk and said, 'Excuse me, do you mind if I ask you a question?'

'Not at all,' replied the monk.

'I am travelling from the village in the mountains to the village in the valley and I was wondering if you knew what it is like in the village in the valley?'

'Tell me,' said the monk. 'What was your experience of the village in the mountains?'

'Dreadful,' replied the traveller. 'To be honest I am glad to be away from there. I found the people most unwelcoming. When I first arrived I was greeted coldly. I was never made to feel a part of the village no matter how hard I tried. The villagers keep very much to themselves, they don't take kindly to strangers. So tell me, what can I expect in the village in the valley?'

'I'm sorry to tell you,' said the monk, 'but I think your experience will be much the same there.' The traveller hung his head despondently and walked on.

A few months later another traveller was journeying down the same road and he also came upon the monk. 'Good day,' said the traveller.

'Good day,' said the monk.

'How are you?' asked the traveller.

'I'm well,' replied the monk. 'Where are you going?'

'I'm going to the village in the valley,' replied the traveller. 'Do you know what it is like?'

'I do,' replied the monk. 'But first, tell me — where have you come from?'

'I've come from the village in the mountains.'

'And how was that?'

'It was a wonderful experience. I would have stayed if I could but I am committed to travelling on. I felt as though I were a member of the family in the village. The elders gave me much advice, the children laughed and joked with me and the people generally were kind and generous. I am sad to have left there. It will always hold special memories for me. And what of the village in the valley?' he asked again.

'I think you will find it much the same,' replied the monk. 'Good day to you.'

'Good day and thank you,' replied the traveller, smiled and journeyed on.

1.2 Filters on Your World

Have you ever bought a car and realised how suddenly you become aware of all the other cars of the same type on the road? Or have you ever had an experience, maybe an insight about yourself, only to discover that many of your friends, previously unbeknown to you, have had the same or a similar experience? Do you see the wine glass as half full as opposed to half empty by looking for what is there as opposed to what is not? These are examples of ways you filter what happens to you so that you let some information in and keep other information out.

Different filters
　　Here is an example conversation that highlights the need to be able to understand and relate to different filters.

When Janet and Bill had a conversation, each found the other frustrating. Janet liked to discuss the details of what was needed whereas Bill preferred to discuss the broader strategic concepts. For example, Janet would say, 'I'd like Peter to go to the next meeting,' and Bill would reply 'We haven't decided on the main areas of the plan that didn't work.' Janet's conversation centred on future actions whereas Bill concentrated more on the past. Janet would pay attention to the similarities between one situation and another — 'This is like another idea I have about what we might do to improve the office layout.' Bill would concentrate on the exception by saying things like, 'No this is different' or 'We didn't include an overall plan.' It was as if Janet and Bill were talking a different language. They had different filters on their experience. They didn't find meetings with each other easy!

Two people using the same filters in conversation helps to build rapport. If the filters that you use are different to the ones used by your partner then, as with Janet and Bill, you may experience discord and frustration. By using similar patterns, in this case language patterns, to your partner you are increasing the chances of creating a climate of rapport and trust.

Flexibility

Learning to recognise the filters that you and others use is a first step. Developing your flexibility in the way you use the filters gives you choice — choice about responses you want in yourself and in others. There must be hundreds of filters that we use every day to translate experience into perception. This section outlines some of the ones that can have the most value in applications of NLP and some of the ones that have the most impact at work.

In our example, for Bill to build rapport and thereby his understanding with Janet he could have replied in the following vein:

Janet   'I'd like Peter to go to the next meeting.'
Bill   'Yes, Peter would make some useful contributions. Let's note that so when we have decided what areas of the plan didn't work we can also decide who else we might want to include.'
Janet   'This is like another idea I have about what we might do to improve the office layout.'
Bill   'You usually come up with lots of ideas, Janet. Let's discuss them and include my idea about the overall plan.'

ASSOCIATED/DISSOCIATED

Think of a conversation you had recently with one of your colleagues. As you think of this conversation pay attention to how you are thinking about it. For example, are you seeing, hearing and feeling the situation as if you are in your own body, i.e. seeing it out of your own eyes, hearing it with your own ears and experiencing the feelings of being there? Or are you experiencing the situation as if you are outside your own body, i.e. seeing yourself in the situation, hearing yourself as if you were an observer? The experience of being in your own body is what is referred to as **associated** and the experience of being outside your own body is known as **dissociated**.

Pay attention for a moment to your surroundings. You may begin to notice what you see around you, the quality of the light, the colours and shapes, the shadows and the clarity of the scene. As you notice the scene you may begin to hear sounds close to you and farther away. As you become aware of even more sounds, turn your conscious mind towards them. Be aware of the location of the sounds, their loudness or softness, their tone and speed. You may find yourself becoming aware of what you can feel, of the textures and pressures that you feel on your body. Sense those parts of you that are touching the ground or a chair. Allow yourself to notice any smells or tastes that you experience. And as you do this pay attention to the feelings within you, to any tensions or internal emotions, their precise location and intensity. This awareness of yourself through all of your senses is an associated state.

Now step back or stand behind the chair in which you were sitting and see yourself sitting or standing as you were a moment ago. Look at yourself so that you can see the whole of you. Notice how the you 'there' interacts with the environment. Be aware of how the you 'there' in front of you looks and sounds. In this dissociated state you will be detached from the feelings.

The ability to associate and dissociate is an important NLP skill. To experience the emotions and feelings of a situation fully you need to be associated. However, to distance yourself from the emotions as you might wish to do in dealing with the reality or memory of a traumatic situation, you would need to be able to dissociate. One of our course delegates was responsible for the counselling and support of fire crew and wanted to be able to teach them to dissociate from traumatic memories as a way of managing and diminishing stress.

Dealing with stress

Dissociation is a way of detaching yourself from the emotions of a situation and develops your ability to receive feedback. Chapter 3.2 of the Toolkit, Receive Feedback Constructively, gives you the steps to do this.

The skill lies in using associated and dissociated states for a purpose in a way that works for you rather than always being affected emotionally by what happens to you, or remaining untouched by experiences.

TOWARDS/AWAY FROM

Think of a goal that you have for yourself right now. It can be a personal goal or a work goal. It can be short or long term. Be aware of how you are thinking about this goal. Are you imagining what it would be like to achieve the goal, i.e. what you are seeing, hearing and feeling? Or are you aware of what stops you and what you don't want? For example, if you are thinking of slimming, do you imagine yourself slim and fit or do you think of the food you want to avoid and the weight you want to lose? What is in your mind? Your ability to think about what you really do want is known as **towards** thinking. Your ability to think about what you don't want is known as **away from** thinking.

Don't worry!

This concept of towards/away from is explained further in Chapter 2.2. In the context of goal setting, people who think 'towards' are more likely to achieve what they do want. Those who think of what they don't want are likely to achieve just that. For example, if you tell yourself not to worry you are effectively programming yourself to worry. If you think about being confident, that is what you are more likely to become.

MATCH/MISMATCH

Look at the shapes below and describe their relationship to each other.

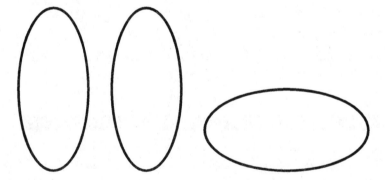

What do you notice? Do you notice in what ways they are similar, i.e. they are all oval, or do you notice that two are upright and one is on its side? In effect, do you look for what is the same (**match**) or do you look for what is different (**mismatch**)?

When meeting someone for the first time a person who sorts for a match might think of similar people, similar situations or how the other is like them. Someone who sorts for a mismatch will identify what is different about this person and this situation compared with others they know and themselves.

Job profiles

Certain professions train people to think in a particular way. For example, I have come across more mismatching patterns of thinking in professions associated with information technology and finance than I have in many other fields of business. There is no right or wrong. Certain jobs depend on a person's ability to match, just as some depend on an ability to mismatch. A software engineer trained to uncover system 'bugs' may be skilled at mismatching, looking for what doesn't fit, as indeed will someone in accounting whose job it is to find the imbalance. What matters is how appropriately these skills are used. If used appropriately they are fine, if not they can cause problems. The 'yes, but' pattern in conversation is an example of mismatching.

'I'm really pleased with the way this project has gone.'

'Yes, but there's a danger we're going to get over-confident.'

'You're right. Let's review objectively what we've achieved so that we build some of the good practices into future projects.'

'That's all very well, but we don't have the time right now.'

'Well, how about putting a date in the diary in a few weeks' time?'

'That's easy to say but not so easy in practice. Things change so rapidly around here.'

Dealing with this in conversation can be hard work unless you are another mismatcher who enjoys a good argument!

BIG CHUNK/SMALL CHUNK

Look around you at the room you are in. How would you describe it to someone who has never seen it before? Do you pay attention to things such as spaciousness, feel, style? Or do you pay attention to number of windows, colour of furnishings, the details? Is it a mix of both? The spaciousness, feel and style are examples of **big chunk** thinking, whereas the details are **small chunk**.

This pattern of thinking can apply to anything. For example, if you have set a specific goal for yourself you could **chunk up** to more global goals or **chunk down** to milestones which you could set along the way. In most work situations the application of big chunk/small chunk thinking is equally relevant.

Let's suppose you are in a cookery class. You need an orange for the dish you are preparing. Another member of the class also needs an orange, but there is only one. Without flexibility in thinking the usual solution would be to accept the facts as they appear and cut the orange in half, taking one half each. If, however, you 'chunk up' in relation to your needs in the situation by asking 'What do you need the orange for?', you will discover broader needs. For example, you might want the orange for a cake and your colleague may want the orange for a soufflé. If you 'chunk down' on the request for the orange by asking 'What specifically do you need for your soufflé?', you might discover that the other person needs just the pulp. You know that you only need the skin, the zest, for your cake. It is possible for you both to have exactly what you want.

This skill of chunking up and chunking down is the essence of skilled negotiation. It opens the doors to the likelihood of achieving a win/win position, in which both parties achieve all they want.

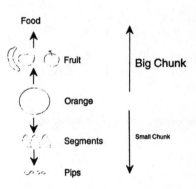

PAST/PRESENT/FUTURE

Where in time do you put your attention? Some people live their lives in the past, thinking about what has gone before. Some people live for the moment, and their attention is on the present. Some are constantly planning and thinking about the future. You may have experienced these kinds of questions that look to the future:

- 'What's for dinner?'

- 'How long till we get home?'

- 'Where are we going on holiday?'

- 'What's next on the agenda?'

- 'What I want to achieve by the end of the project is…'

Or you may know someone who concentrates on the past:

- 'What did you say earlier?'

- 'Did you see what that person was wearing?'

- 'Do you remember when we were on holiday?'

- 'The last meeting we had was important.'

There is no right or wrong, no good or bad, but this does have implications for how people communicate with each other. A friend called to invite me to a school reunion to talk over old times. As someone whose attention is more on the present and the future, the thought of reminiscing about the past didn't strike me as an attractive proposition!

ACTIVITY/PERSON/OBJECT/PLACE/TIME

Think of the best meal you ever had.

Your memory of this will be determined by the filter you use. For example, if you sort by:

activity you recall what you and others did at this meal. Maybe you had a memorable conversation or the waiter dropped the plates;

person you remember the meal in relation to who was there;

object your memories are associated with possibly the food, a present you were given, the pictures in the restaurant, the type of furniture;

place your memories are of the location — the restaurant, the town, the country or possibly the location of the table at which you sat;

time you remember the time and date, an anniversary or another special occasion. You might remember that it was the first day of your new job or a farewell dinner at the end of term.

INTERNAL/EXTERNAL

How do you know when you've done a good job? Which of the following responses would be most likely to be true for you?

I know I've done a good job when:

- I see people using the results of what I have produced;

- I feel good inside;

- I know I've met the standards I set myself;

- we get more orders;

- I can say to myself, 'That was a job well done.'

Externally referenced people rely on external sources for their evidence of fulfilment. For example, they rely on what other people say and do. They may also rely on external factors such as 'more orders', or 'people use the results of what has been produced'.

Internally referenced people use their own internal feelings, images and voices as their evidence of fulfilment. Your preference here will make a big difference to the way you work. If you are externally referenced you may be more likely to depend on having others around you. If, however, you are internally referenced then you are independent of external people and events.

Dependence and independence

People who are independent in style are usually internally referenced. This is a characteristic pattern of senior managers. They can be concerned about what happens outside themselves — they need to be! However, they do not depend on external circumstances to feel satisfied. Can you imagine a managing director who *depended* on having his staff tell him that he was doing OK? Some of the leading figures of our time have succeeded because of their ability to persevere despite the external feedback they have received.

CONVINCER PATTERN

I was explaining to a client how he might restructure his management team. He seemed unsure although he accepted the principle of what I was saying. We discussed the plans in a number of different ways. I eventually reflected back to him his uncertainty. He replied, 'I just don't see it, Sue.' At that point I drew it on the whiteboard. 'Now I'm sure it will work,' he said.

Everyone has a specific means by which they become convinced. In this client's case the principal factor was that he needed to see the ideas visually before he was convinced that they would work. So part of what makes someone convinced is the channel through which they receive the information.

Other people might equally well have been convinced by:

- hearing what I had to say;

- trying it out to find out if it worked in practice;

- reading the plan in more detail.

Making decisions

There are differences in the way people need to receive information within these broader categories. Some people need to be told a number of times or have a number of examples before they are convinced. Others need to be convinced over a period of time — time is the deciding factor for them. Some people make decisions on the bare outlines of the facts — they don't need the detail in order to be convinced; yet others need to have it proved to them time and time again. They will be convinced but only for one situation and one context at a time.

If your job involves you in having to convince others in order to achieve the result you want, then you need to know the pattern by which they operate. You can then match this pattern in the way you present your information.

To find out more about the filters you use, refer to the questionnaire in Chapter 3.3 of the Toolkit, Identify Your Filters.

SUMMARY

The filters on your experience determine how you make sense of reality. Nature has shown us that it is those animals and plants that have learned to cooperate with each other and their environment that survive. By learning to recognise these filters in yourself and others, you begin to build bridges of communication. There are no rights and wrongs about the filters and there are many more than the ones I have covered here. Your filters can vary over time and context, and they are a part of what makes you unique.

THOUGHT PROVOKERS

Read the following passages and determine which filters are being used by each author.

1   I'm someone who enjoys life to the full. I play squash, I write, I work full time as a salesperson and I have a young family who keep me busy in any spare time I have! I get a lot of satisfaction from what I do. I set myself goals and I know by my own standards when I have achieved them. I enjoy travel, particularly to Europe, and I love eating out.

---

2   I can be a difficult person, or so others tell me. I can usually see the alternative point of view. I enjoy a good discussion, some would say argument. I like perfection. If something isn't quite right it irritates me. I spend a lot of time working and I am meticulous in the way I go about that. I am a programmer and the work I do requires attention to detail and the ability to see immediately if something is wrong.

3   I am a good listener. People come to me with their problems. I have always had this sort of role, not only in my work life but also with my friends. I have spent most of my life in the same part of England. I have always liked the people here. I can recall some very special occasions that I have spent with friends in the past. I have always been a bit indecisive about what I might do next. I have always let others push me into new situations or jobs, and have tended only to change if I have been dissatisfied with what I was doing at the time.

One of our course delegates was recounting an incident which occurred with his 3-year-old daughter.

'How many times do I have to tell you to put your toys away?', he asked her.

'Four times,' she replied categorically.

Linguistic

The power of language

Your language is your life. Your language is an embroidery of patterns of words that tell your story. Your language is either your gateway to learning and choice or your jailer.

In business especially language is a powerful tool. It is the currency of business transactions. By learning to develop mastery of your language you can:

- improve the quality of the information you exchange with others;
- increase the level of understanding you create with your communication;
- influence the outcomes of situations;
- empower yourself and others by challenging the constraints that show themselves in language;
- bypass conscious resistance by engaging the unconscious mind;
- communicate in a way that is captivating and compelling;
- enrich your language and consequently enrich your life.

The opportunity to practise your skills with language is available to you not only when you interact with others, but also when you interact with yourself.

1.3 Enriched Communication

Personal success relies largely on your ability to communicate. What you say matters little compared with how you say it. To communicate with influence it is important to be able to use the language that engages the hearts and minds of your listeners.

One of the early discoveries in NLP was that skilled communicators used language in a way that created a climate of trust and understanding. The difference that made the difference was in the speaker's instinctive ability to adapt their language to match the language of the person to whom they were speaking. This way of building rapport through language is explained in Chapter 2.3.

A study of powerful communicators also revealed that they naturally use language that is rich in its use of all the senses. For example:

> A *lover's eyes will gaze an eagle blind;*
> A *lover's ears will hear the lowest sound,*
> *When the suspicious head of theft is stopp'd:*
> *Love's feeling is more soft and sensible*
> *Than are the tender horns of cockled snails:*
> *Love's tongue proves dainty Bacchus gross in taste.*
>
> **Love's Labour's Lost**, William Shakespeare

It is reassuring to know that you don't have to be Shakespeare to write and speak with compelling, enriched language. I first came across NLP when I attended a course in creative writing more than nine years ago. I wanted to be able to write with interest and style. The course I attended was run by two people, one an author, the other a consultant who had 'coded' the writing skills of this author in order that we might reproduce some of his writing style for ourselves. I became curious about this process of coding talent. Therein lies the story of how I came to be interested in NLP.

Business language

The point about this is that you can 'code' the writing or speaking style of any great communicator. It sometimes seems that the qualities of compelling communication have been stripped away to leave the bare, cold, neutral language that fills so many hours of business presentations and so many pages of reports. By studying the difference that makes the difference between the people to whom you are more likely to give your attention and the ones whose reports you shove to the bottom of the pile, you will uncover the secret of enriched communication.

Studying the Shakespearian passage you will find that it contains language that appeals to the eyes, the ears and the feelings. Of course, you may not want to communicate exactly like Shakespeare in one of your project review meetings, but you do probably want to capture and hold your audience's attention. And you do probably want to speak or write in a way that increases the likelihood of your listener or your reader understanding what you say.

All senses

To do this it is important to be able to have the choice of using all the senses in the way you speak or write. You will discover that your listeners and your readers have preferences. For example:

Pete and Joe rarely agreed. They each complained that they found the other frustrating. As senior managers in a rapidly growing organisation it was vital that they understood each other's point of view. Whenever they got together to make decisions Pete wanted to get a grasp of the situation and make decisions based on his gut feeling. He'd had a lot of success working this way. Joe, on the other hand, liked to talk his ideas through in full. Typically he would have a list of points that he wanted to discuss. Pete quickly got frustrated with this and usually cut the meeting short. Their inability to reach a satisfactory conclusion had resulted in Pete's moving Joe to a new position where they had less direct contact.

It seemed as though Pete and Joe were speaking a different language, and in a way they were. Pete thought and talked mainly in terms of feelings. He made decisions based on his 'gut feel'. Joe had a very auditory way of communicating — he would 'talk his ideas through' and have 'points to discuss'. They were using different senses to communicate with each other, or rather to try to communicate with each other.

SENSORY SPECIFIC LANGUAGE

If your means of communicating is the same as the person you are speaking to, then you are talking the same language, so to speak! If, however, like Pete and Joe you use different systems to communicate, then you will both have difficulty understanding and accepting what the other has to say.

Your speech is an expression of the way you think. For example, if you think visually you are more likely to say:

- 'I get the picture.'

- 'It's clear now.'

- 'I see what you mean.'

because you do!

If, however, you think in an auditory way you would be more likely to say:

- 'That sounds good.'

- 'It rings bells for me.'

- 'I hear what you are saying.'

If your experience is more feelings based then you would be likely to say:

- 'That feels right.'

- 'It made an impact on me.'

- 'I was moved by what you said.'

The language of taste and smell also comes into this category of feelings:

- 'It left a bad taste in my mouth.'

- 'I smelt something fishy.'

Some of the key words for each of the three systems are:

Visual	Auditory	Feelings
see	sound	impact
focus	hear	taste
clear	tell	feel
bright	say	touch
picture	click	smell
hazy	bang	tense
colour	talk	rough
view	volume	bitter
dim	loud	relaxed
look	snap	whiff

Some of the key expressions for each of the three systems are:

Visual

Things are a bit hazy
I take a dim view of that
The future is looking brighter
The outlook is bleak
Seeing things through rose coloured glasses
He is in a black mood today
We're in the pink
I look forward to seeing you
Things are looking up
We've a clear way forward
That was a colourful expression

Auditory

I tell myself to take care
I'm glad to hear it
Tell me how it is
My teeth are chattering
Things clicked into place
Let me explain
We're in harmony
Listen to yourself
We're in tune with each other
It was music to my ears
I'm pleased you said that

Feelings

Racked with pain
The sweet smell of success
Get in touch with reality
A taste of fear
I've got a grasp of what you mean
Warm regards

I've got a handle on it
I was moved
It was a blow to my pride
Let's firm up on this
I savoured the moment
Hold on

Excellent communicators naturally use the system preferred by the person to whom they are speaking, at least initially. This ensures that they are talking the same language and are more easily understood than if they were to use a representational system that was disliked by their listener.

> *Ships that pass in the night, and speak each other in passing;*
> *Only a signal shown and a distant voice in the darkness;*
> *So on the ocean of life we pass and speak one another,*
> *Only a look and a voice; then darkness again and a silence.*
>
> *'The Theologian's Tale: Elizabeth',*
> *Henry Wadsworth Longfellow*

> *You'd scarce expect one of my age*
> *To speak in public on the stage;*
> *And if I chance to fall below*
> *Demosthenes or Cicero,*
> *Don't view me with a critic's eye*
> *But pass my imperfections by.*
> *Large streams from little fountains flow,*
> *Tall oaks from little acorns grow.*
>
> *'Lines Written for a School Declamation', David Everett*

These, I believe, are examples of compelling, inspiring speakers. By developing your ability to use all sensory systems in your language, you will be developing your ability to communicate in a way that is interesting and compelling.
   Contrast the following:

Captivating language

As you walk down the corridor to the main office you will see a pink notice on the wall to the side of the EXIT door. Read this — it will remind you of the emergency procedures we have demonstrated this morning.

This has a very different effect to saying:

Be sure to take account of the emergency procedures on the way out.

The first example is more to likely to engage the listener's attention. It uses sensory specific language, and it is therefore

likely to be more memorable.
  Compare:

Neutral

Things have been difficult for some time now. As a result of this our objective for the next period is to introduce a quality programme. It will be crucial to the future success of the company. By giving attention to quality we will be understanding and meeting the requirements of our customers, both internal and external. I cannot stress the importance of this enough.

with:

Enriched

For the last year our sales and it seems our spirit in this team has fallen. Because of what I feel to be the problem and because you tell me that our focus of attention now needs to be different, I have written out my thoughts for our outcomes for the year to come. I would like to explain these to you; I'd like you to listen and ask yourself, 'How can I make this work for me?' I want to hear the answers to this question. My vision of the future is one where each of the people — staff and clients alike — with whom we come into contact will see a new image emerging, one that communicates attention and care and concern that we really meet their needs. I believe we can do this by ensuring that we see each and every one of them to ask them all, 'What do you really need from us in order for you to feel that you are being served well?' and 'What would have to be true for you to want to continue to keep us as your main supplier for the next three years?' We will know when we have achieved our goal when our customers invite us to meet with them to discuss their needs and when they say, 'You understand us and demonstrate that you will act to ensure our needs are met.'

Each style of communication has its place. Unfortunately, the neutral, abstract language is often used in business through habit rather than choice. If you choose to increase understanding, motivate and inspire, then enriched communication is the way to do it.

SUMMARY

Enriched communication is the essence of motivation and commitment. Appeal to the eyes, ears and feelings of your listeners and you have their understanding and their attention. Inspirational leaders throughout history have instinctively had the ability to capture the hearts and minds of their audience. By understanding the components of enriched language you too can now inspire and delight your listeners. Bring your business meetings and presentations alive with your skilled use of language.

THOUGHT PROVOKERS

1   For someone you haven't met before, how could you prepare to present your ideas so that you ensured that each of the visual/auditory/feelings systems are taken account of?

2   Rewrite these sentences using enriched language:
    a.   It is important to me that I progress within this organisation.
    b.   I want to know what we aim to achieve with this meeting.

3   Select someone with whom you work. Listen to the language he or she uses. Identify any preferences for visual/auditory/feelings systems.

4   How can you ensure that you address each of the senses when giving a presentation?
    a.   Visual.
    b.   Auditory.
    c.   Feelings.

Gregory Bateson was one of the influences on John Grinder and Richard Bandler. Much of his thinking about change and learning has been incorporated and developed in the concepts of NLP. Some of his discoveries about learning came from the time he spent studying porpoises. Some of this work involved watching porpoises in performances for the general public.

In particular the audiences were shown how a porpoise learned to do a trick. As the porpoise circled in the pool the trainer would wait and watch for the porpoise to do something different — flipping its tail or spinning around. As soon as it did this different behaviour, and it didn't really matter what it was as long as it was different, the trainer would blow a whistle and give the porpoise a fish. As soon as the porpoise repeated the behaviour the trainer would once again blow a whistle and give the porpoise another fish. In this way the porpoise learned what it had to do to get its reward and would demonstrate the new behaviour in order to obtain the fish.

There were usually several shows each day so at the next show naturally the porpoise would swim out into the pool and begin to demonstrate the new behaviour that had previously earned the fish. Of course, this time the trainer wanted to demonstrate to the audience how the porpoise learned new tricks and consequently didn't give it the fish. The porpoise would become increasingly frustrated and towards the end of the show would do something else — jump out of the water, for example. As soon as it demonstrated this new behaviour the trainer would blow the whistle and give it a fish. The porpoise quickly realised that this was what it needed to do and would continue to jump out of the water, and each time it did so the trainer blew the whistle and gave it a fish.

At each subsequent show the same pattern was repeated — the porpoise getting increasingly frustrated each time until in desperation it performed a new behaviour by chance, at which point the trainer immediately blow the whistle and gave it a fish. The frustration in the porpoise increased to such a point that occasionally the trainer would break the procedure and give the porpoise a fish without it demonstrating a new behaviour.

Eventually after many shows the porpoise seemed to change dramatically and became very excited as it was waiting to be let into the show pool. When it was released into the pool the porpoise put on an amazing performance that included eight completely new behaviours, some of which had never been witnessed before.

When asked about the unearned fish the trainer replied, 'Those fish were to maintain my relationship with the porpoise. Only by maintaining our relationship can we communicate in this way and achieve the kind of results you have just seen.'

Precision Questions *1.4*

One of the fashionable words in organisations today is **empowerment**. Empowerment is the process of tapping into and utilising your own and others' full potential. The challenge is how to achieve this. NLP, and specifically the questioning skills developed by John Grinder and Richard Bandler, provide a way to empower yourself and others. Empowerment starts within. It starts with your ability to take responsibility for your own experience. This is what 'ownership' is all about.

One day on holiday in Dorset with my sons we were joined by another little boy. He and my son Alex decided to build a sandcastle. When they were doing this I overheard them talking about school. Alex asked him what he liked doing best at school. 'I don't know,' he replied, 'I'm not very clever.' He was 6 years old and his words reflected a choice he had made or had learned already that would affect his potential for the future.

The linguist Noam Chomsky distinguished between two levels of language:

surface structure this is everything you say either to yourself or to other people;

deep structure the deep meaning of what you say containing information neither expressed nor known consciously.

Ownership and empowerment

A number of things can happen between the deep structure and the surface structure of the language. The intention of the communication may be lost or changed in the process of converting one to the other.

LAZY LANGUAGE

Look at the following expressions. Read them quickly.

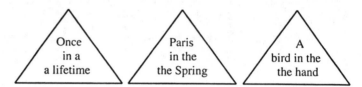

What do they say? Now read the following passage. How many ʃs are there?

FEATURE FILMS ARE THE RESULT OF YEARS OF SCIENTIFIC STUDY COMBINED WITH THE EXPERIENCE OF YEARS

Deletion, distortion and generalisation

The expressions actually read Once in *a a* lifetime, A bird in *the the* hand, Paris in *the the* Spring. We often distort what we read and hear and see to fit in with our expectations. In the passage there are 6 ʃs — if you got both of these right, well done!

These simple exercises illustrate the sort of processes that occur in our thinking. We delete, distort and generalise information so that it becomes disconnected from its deeper meaning. We typically use an imprecise form of language in speech — a lazy language. This lazy language becomes characteristic of many business problems.

For example:

Do you have a 'they' in your company? I have worked with many different companies and I have discovered that there is one cause of all the problems: 'they'.

They...!

- They *don't communicate effectively;*
- They *introduce changes without consultation;*
- They *don't listen;*
- They *expect you to know what's going on;*
- They *keep you in the dark.*

They *are very elusive*, I *have discovered*. They *are never in the same room as the people who are talking about them*. They *are very often one or two levels higher in the management structure, even when the people referring to them in one case were the board of directors themselves!*

The 'they' syndrome illustrates the tendency of those people who use this form of speech to put the source of problems and therefore the possibility of change outside themselves. The 'they' being so elusive and so impossible to pin down means that they (the person talking!) can avoid change because the source of that change is out of their grasp.

John Grinder and Richard Bandler made a study of these language patterns.

They developed and refined a set of questions designed to challenge and influence the constraints that people put on themselves. These questions are designed to reconnect the speaker with his or her experience and are influential in triggering change, and are discussed in the rest of this chapter.

However, a word of warning. These questions can be experienced as intimidating and aggressive if used without regard for the person you are questioning. Before using the questions on anyone other than yourself, I encourage you to read the section on building and maintaining rapport, Chapter 2.3, so that you maintain the trust and respect of the person on the receiving end of the questions.

DELETIONS

Deletions are examples of language where parts of the meaning have been omitted.

VAGUE SUBJECTS

This is where 'they' come into their own. 'They don't tell you what's going on round here,' 'They overlooked me in the recent promotions.' Who exactly are they? I realise that this is the million dollar question. When I get the answer to this one I will have answered the question to many companies' problems. The point is that 'they' is a way of avoiding responsibility and ownership. 'They' is an example of a vague subject.

This language pattern implies that the speaker has no influence over what is happening around them. Other examples of this are:

People don't let you make decisions.   Which people
exactly?

| Customers make life very difficult. | Which customers are you referring to? |
| I don't agree. | With what or with whom? |

These kinds of question reconnect the speaker with their thinking about the source of their problems. It also gives you specific information rather than leaving you to guess or mind-read who is implied by the statement.

VAGUE ACTIONS

'She ignored me.' You could guess what is meant by this and you would probably be wrong. The question to ask is, 'How exactly did she ignore you?'. Your aim in asking this question is to find out exactly what behaviour the speaker experienced to lead them to conclude that 'she ignored them'. The speaker is evaluating the behaviour in a way that may not be true. In this case 'ignored' is a vague action.

So the question 'How did she ignore you?' or 'How specifically did he/she/they do that?' challenges the way you and others interpret and evaluate actions.

Appraisal action plans seem to spawn vague actions:

- Fred needs to *improve* his time management skills.

- Jane will *build* on her experience as a sales executive.

- We are going to *develop* Harry's ability to delegate.

Such statements are often 'cop outs', a way of avoiding thinking about how exactly the manager and the job holder will bring these changes about. Not surprisingly many of the suggested changes don't happen. When challenged the next most popular 'cop out' statement is, 'We are going to send him/her on a course!'

COMPARISONS

'We are going to build a better world.' Better than what exactly?

Performance objectives and measures of job success often seem to contain this kind of comparison.

Fewer customer complaints.	Fewer than what?
More sales leads.	More than what or than whom?
Better management communication.	Better than what, precisely?

Comparative words include more, less, better, worse, fewer, well, badly — anything that suggests an evaluation against some yardstick. The difficulty in understanding what is meant by these occurs when the yardstick is omitted.

'That was a brilliant report.'
'My presentation was a disaster.' } Compared with what?
'The company is doing well.'

Abstractions take the action out of life. As a language pattern an abstraction immobilises the owner of the words. You are probably very familiar with these examples:

ABSTRACTIONS

- communication

- discussion

- relationships

- action

- empowerment!

- abstraction!!

Abstractions are a way of taking a verb, an action word, and turning it into a noun, a thing, an *abstract* thing. This is called 'nominalisation'. In doing so you take away the action.
    For example:

'We have problems with our communication.'

'How do you want to be able to communicate differently?' would be a way of introducing the possibility of the speaker beginning to move forward to a way of developing new skills.

To test for an abstraction, if you can put 'ongoing' in front of the word, e.g ongoing communication, ongoing relationship, it is probably an abstraction.
    The way to challenge an abstraction is to question to find out who is doing what and how. For example, if someone says 'It was a difficult conversation,' your question could be, 'Who was talking to whom and how was it difficult?'

This kind of statement occurs when the speaker expresses an

OPINIONS AS FACTS

opinion as if it were a truth by deleting the fact that it 's an opinion.

● 'This is the right way to do the job.'

● 'It's bad to be inconsistent.'

'According to whom?' is the key question.

This sort of statement can be received as aggressive. An alternative way to express the same thing would be to say:

● I *believe* this is the right way to do the job.

● *Joe thinks* it's bad to be inconsistent.

Opinions as facts are value judgements, characteristic of people who believe that their 'map of the world' is the right one. The owners of such statements have closed the door to the possibility that there are other opinions, other ways to do things. Asking the question 'According to whom?' reconnects them with their personal ownership of these views.

They may discover that the owner is someone from their past, their parents or teachers. 'It's wrong to leave food on your plate.' 'I wants don't get.' 'Children should be seen and not heard.' According to whom? Certainly not the children in the last example! These kinds of statement are the expression of beliefs.

GENERALISATIONS

Generalisations exist when you take specific experiences and generalise them to make them true outside their particular context. In so doing you distort your experience.

Sometimes it is important to do this. You need generalisations as referents in language, otherwise you would have to go into a tremendous amount of detail when you speak. However, generalisations can be misleading.

UNIVERSAL STATEMENTS

● 'I always catch a cold in the winter.'

● 'No one ever tells you what is going on around here.'

Universal statements consist of words such as no one, everyone, never, always, all, nothing. The speaker has generalised specific experiences to make them true in *all* circumstances. One way of responding would be to use the generalisation back to them as a question:

- 'Always?'

- 'No one?'

Alternative ways of responding would be to challenge the detail behind the statement:

- 'She never listens to me.'

- 'How do you know that?'

- 'Has there ever been a time when she did listen to you?'

These challenges reconnect the speaker with the reality of their experience.

I was recently in discussion with a friend of mine who works as a personal assistant. In this role she provides administrative support for a team of senior managers. She had attended one of our courses and had shown a high level of skill in her ability to coach and facilitate others. I was discussing the possibility of how she might use these skills to help the management team introduce the changes they had talked about.

'Oh, I can't do that,' she immediately replied. In fact she had several 'can'ts in relation to herself. At some level she had chosen to limit her potential.

STOPPERS AND LIMITERS

Can you imagine the managing director of a company or the head of a country saying 'I can't' when asked to consider the future? They wouldn't last in that position for long.

Faced with 'I can't', what can you say? 'What stops you?' is one choice. This invites the speaker to identify and face up to the reality of the obstacles, imagined or otherwise.

Another possibility is to ask, 'What would happen if you did?' This is a very powerful question. In its own right it can empower people to go beyond the barriers they build for themselves. However, when you ask the question, pay attention to whether the speaker really answers it in their thinking and in their speech. You may find they answer spontaneously with comments such as, 'Well I just can't', indicating that they haven't really considered the question. However, if you ask the question in a way that encourages them to consider the possibility — 'I know you can't but what would happen if you did use your skills to help the management team?' — then the other person has to imagine what that would be like in order to answer the question.

Eye movements, explained in Chapter 1.1, give you clues about whether someone is processing the question or not. If they answer with an unblinking immediate 'I can't', it is unlikely that they have processed the question. However, if they look away or even defocus, looking straight ahead, then some processing is taking place. Once they have done that they have gone beyond the barrier.

Influence through questions

What we know is that once a possibility is imagined it opens the door to it becoming reality. When you use this kind of question you are influencing the possibility of the idea becoming the outcome. Questions are powerful influencers because they invite the listener's mind to participate in finding an answer. Questions are inescapable.

DRIVERS

Drivers are statements of need. 'I have to finish this article,' 'I must tidy my desk,' 'I should go and visit my friend.' None of these statements implies that the speaker really wants to do any of these things.

For most people 'musts', 'shoulds', 'oughts' and 'have tos' are accompanied by a feeling of tension. 'I must tidy my desk.' 'I should go and visit my friend.' These words are characteristic of 'driven' behaviours, often 'driven' by someone else even if that is someone from your past, a parent or a teacher perhaps. Maybe they were the ones who believed that you must keep your desk tidy.

Outcomes containing words such as 'must', 'should' or 'ought' lose their power because the words suggest outcomes that belong to someone else. Your true outcomes contain words such as 'really want to' and 'can'. The words you use are an expression of your experience. They trigger off very different types of feeling, which will in turn influence your potential and your ability to succeed in achieving what you really want.

DISTORTIONS

Distortions are examples of language where the owner of the words has distorted their experience. It may be that they have made faulty connections between different parts of their experience.

BLAMERS

- 'You make me angry.'

- 'This company demotivates me.'

The owner of this sort of statement has given the responsibility for their state and feelings to others. They have become dependent on their environment and have surrendered their choice to feel the way they want to feel. It is not that these statements aren't true; they are. But the speaker has allowed others to affect them.

The challenge:

- 'How is it possible for me to make you angry?'

- 'How does the company demotivate you?'

The question encourages the other person to consider exactly how that happens. Once they begin to understand the structure of this experience they begin to have a choice. They may still choose to feel angry, but they will own that anger once they begin to say 'I feel angry', rather than 'You make me angry'. Instead of giving power to others for their feelings they restore power to themselves.

- 'I know why you did that.'

- 'She only said that because she was annoyed with me.'

- 'You're upset, I can tell.'

'MIND-READING'

These are examples of the speaker presuming to know what others are thinking or feeling. They are interpretations. For example, it would be more accurate to say, 'You interrupted that customer before they had finished speaking and you kept your arms folded throughout the conversation', than 'You were obviously annoyed with that customer.' The former is specific whereas the latter implies a value judgement.

'How do you know that?' enables the speaker to reconnect their interpretation of others' behaviour back to the behaviour itself. It challenges the assumptions that the speaker is making. It encourages them to be specific in their observations and in their feedback.

INTERPRETATION

Interpretation is when two statements are linked together in such a way that they are taken to mean the same thing. The statement takes the form 'This means that.'

I remember when I went for a job interview in London many years ago. When I left that interview, if someone had asked me what I thought about the interviewer I'd have said something very similar to, 'He ignored me'. What he actually did was to swing his chair around and look out of the window each time he asked me a question. My belief at the time was, 'He didn't look at me, he isn't interested in me for this job!' What I didn't know then but discovered subsequently, when I joined the department, was that this was how he concentrated on conversation. In his perception he wasn't ignoring me at all.

Other examples of this are:
- 'You are speaking with a sharp tone of voice — you are obviously annoyed with me.'
- 'My manager banged the door open. I knew I'd done something wrong.'
- 'You are not smiling. You are obviously not enjoying yourself.'

Challenge this pattern by asking, 'How does this mean that?'
- 'How does that tone of voice mean that I am annoyed with you?'
- 'How does the fact that your manager banged open the door mean that you had done something wrong?'
- 'How does the fact that I am not smiling mean that I am not enjoying myself?'

MANAGE YOUR INTERNAL DIALOGUE

The language that you use may be what you say openly to others. Equally it can be what you say to yourself internally. You can use the 'precision questions' described above to challenge the internal dialogues and in so doing change your feelings and your experience.

Personal confidence

I was once asked by the technical director of a software development company to help him develop the presentations that he was sometimes asked to give internationally. When he explained what he wanted, I discovered that it wasn't help with the design of the presentation, but help to manage his feelings beforehand. Typically he could not sleep well for at least three weeks prior to the presentation. He often felt physically sick on the morning of the presentation itself.

We began to explore the conversations he had with others and himself related to these presentations. What emerged was this:

'These presentations never go well. They expect me to manage the material and all the technical demonstrations. Giving these talks makes me stressed. I know what people in the audience will think, they'll think

this is all obvious. They'll want to leave. I can't relax. It will be the same experience all over again.'

We discovered a series of deletions, distortions and generalisations in his thinking. Over time we took each of these statements and challenged them in the following way:

His thinking	The challenges
'These presentations never go well.'	Never? Has there ever been a time when one did go well? How well specifically do you want it to go? Which presentations specifically don't go well?
'They expect me to manage the material and all the technical demonstrations.'	Who expects you to manage both? How exactly do you want to be able to manage the presentation? How do you know they expect you to manage both?
'Giving these talks makes me feel stressed.'	How exactly does giving the talks cause you to feel stressed? How do you want to feel?
'I know what people in the audience will think, they'll think this is all obvious, they'll want to leave.'	How do you know that? How can you be sure?
'I can't relax. It will be the same experience all over again.'	What stops you from relaxing? What can you do? How do you want to experience this presentation? What would happen if you did relax?

Bit by bit we unravelled the complex web he had spun for himself. He gradually sorted out what he did want to achieve and how he could manage himself to do that.

Three months later I received this letter from him:

Dear Sue,

I have just returned from giving a presentation in Paris. It was a joy to do. I enjoyed the demonstrations and I particularly enjoyed the questions I got from the audience. The hardware didn't all work perfectly but I used this as an opportunity to show how quickly we could recover problems when they occur. You'll be pleased to know nobody left the presentation — at least not until the end! Most of all in the weeks prior to the presentation I slept well, in fact I think I can safely say my family were pleased to have me around. This was not the case in the past. I actually enjoyed the run up to the presentation and I'm looking forward to the next one. Thank you.

Yours peacefully

John

SUMMARY

Recognising and challenging these speech patterns in yourself and others will not only improve the quality of the way you communicate, it will improve your ability to choose what you really want from life. Skilled communicators have mastery over their language. The more flexibility you have over your language, the more potential influence you have over your experience.

Challenging deletions, distortions and generalisations in language with rapport and when appropriate will reconnect you and others with your experience. These challenges are a way of restoring ownership and they are an elegant way of empowering yourself and others to increase the choices you have available to you. The skill of questioning is a way of clarifying and influencing the relationships that exist between yourself and others.

THOUGHT PROVOKERS

Before you start reading this section take a piece of paper and write down your thinking about your ambitions for yourself and what if anything gets in the way of you achieving them. Do a brain dump — whatever comes to mind write it down. Set yourself a limit of 5 minutes and keep writing whatever comes to mind in that time. When you have read the examples of language patterns you can then turn back to your writing and spot any that are true for you.

1   Re-read the passage you wrote about yourself. What patterns can you detect? Use the questions set out in this chapter to challenge those patterns for yourself.

2   Test your own assumptions. Consider the following statements and note your immediate thoughts.

   a   A friend in a computer software company tells you they have a new managing director. She also says the MD is very young for the job. In your mind how old would he or she be?

   b   A colleague tells you that he is moving to another company and is getting a significant pay increase. He currently earns £30,000 per annum. How much do you imagine the pay increase to be?

   c   Your boss tells you he has an urgent job for you to do. When do you imagine this has to be completed by?

   d   A friend tells you she has just bought an expensive new car. What price range would that fall into in your thinking?

   e   A colleague tells you he is going to take a long holiday. How long do you imagine that to be?

   f   A friend invites you for a long run — how long would that be to you?

   Now ask a colleague, a friend, a member of your family or your boss the same questions. How do your answers compare?

3   Consider for a moment something that you would like to do in the future but haven't done yet. It could be something simple and short term, for example:

   ●   clearing your desk;

   ●   writing a letter to a friend;

   ●   reading a book you have bought;

   ●   giving a colleague some information you promised.

Or it might be on a bigger scale such as:

- learning a language;

- taking the holiday you have always wanted;

- changing jobs;

- starting a family.

Which ones would you put into the category of 'must' or 'should' do? Which ones feel more appropriate when you precede them with words like 'want to' and 'can do'?

Take one of the 'musts' and one of the 'can dos'. In your mind step into the 'must do'. For example, 'I must clean my desk'. What sort of feeling do you get when you say this to yourself?

Now try on the 'can do': 'I can learn French.' Choose your own 'I can' and repeat it to yourself. I can... I can... Say it in a matter of fact, encouraging tone of voice. How do you feel? Usually 'I can' said to yourself in a positive way generates feelings of confidence and enthusiasm. 'I can' is a way of giving yourself permission, of reminding yourself what you can indeed do.

4   To challenge the language patterns in the following statements, what questions would you ask?

a   I can't change the way I am.
b   No one can help me.
c   I know they'll think I'm nervous.
d   He did it deliberately.
e   I'm annoyed because you are late.
f   There is only way to give feedback constructively.
g   My staff don't respond to my directions.
h   This relationship isn't what it should be.
i   I'm upset.
j   You upset me.

There existed a psychotherapist who believed that many of the problems that people brought to him were characterised by the existence of 'fish' in their dreams. One day a client came to him and was discussing the problems he had.

'Tell me', said the psychotherapist, 'did you dream last night?'

'I might have done' replied the client.

'And tell me, in this dream was there a river?'

'I don't think so,' replied the client.

'Well, was there any water, if not a river?'

'Well, I guess there might have been.'

'And was there a pool on the ground?'

'Well, I couldn't be certain but it's possible,' the client replied.

'And in this pool could there have been a fish?'

'Well, I can't rule out the possibility that there might have been a fish.'

'Ah ha,' said the psychotherapist, 'I knew it!'

1.5 Metaphor — the Key to the Unconscious Mind

In previous chapters we have explored how thinking patterns, e.g. visual, auditory and feelings, influence the way you communicate and consequently the effect you have on your listener. We also looked at how the meaning of your communication can go through a process of deletion, distortion or generalisation before it emerges as conversation with yourself and others. The quality of this conversation has an impact on your experience. You probably also use metaphors as a way of thinking, for example you may think of life as 'a bed of roses', work as 'a battle', your leisure time as 'a feast of entertainment'. Whatever the metaphor, it will emerge in the words and expressions that you use and will influence your own and others' experience of conversations and situations.

Metaphors thread their way through everyone's life, from the 'story at bedtime', through the parables in the Bible, to your everyday speech and the way you think of yourself, your business, your life. Most advertisements are a form of metaphor: the skilful ones will be successful in promoting the product. Metaphors can be enchanting, enticing and mesmerising in their style. Their effects may be enlightening and empowering when developed and recounted constructively, making them a jewel to treasure. Used carelessly they can be damaging and disturbing.

Metaphors may be single words, expressions or stories. To understand how to construct and tell a story metaphor is to know how to influence with elegance and respect. Milton Erickson, one of the first people to be 'modelled' by John Grinder and Richard Bandler, was a master of the metaphor. He was also a master of change. The methods he used to bring about change in therapy are just as powerful in influencing change in business.

Elegant influence

An example of one of the stories told by Milton Erickson to explain the way he worked with his clients was this:

One day an unknown horse strayed into the yard of the farm where I lived as a child. No one knew where this horse had come from as it had no markings by which it could have been identified. There was no question of keeping the horse — it must belong to someone.

My father decided to lead it home. He mounted the horse and led it to the road and simply trusted the instinct of the horse to lead itself towards its home. He only intervened when the horse left the road to eat grass or to walk into a field. On these occasions my father would firmly guide it back to the road.

In this way the horse was soon returned to its owner. The owner was very surprised to see his horse once more and asked my father, 'How did you know the horse came from here and belonged to us?'

My father replied, 'I didn't know, the horse knew! All I did was to keep him on the road.'

This story illustrates not only the way Milton Erickson worked with his clients, but also the way most NLP is conducted today. By providing guidance only where needed, NLP respects the fact that you each have all the resources you need to solve your problems. Given the space and the encouragement to use these resources, you are more likely to find solutions that are congruent with who you are, that are compatible with you. These solutions are therefore much more likely to be ones to which you are committed and which therefore will work to produce the outcome you want.

Generating commitment

A director of a company facing closure was confronted with the unenviable task of announcing to one of the divisions that they had to lose half of their workforce in the following two years. This meant making 2000 people redundant. Everyone was apprehensive and tense. Rumours of the cutbacks had already spread throughout the site and it seemed unlikely that the employees would be willing to listen to what the director had to say, let alone participate in the implementation of the cutbacks.

The director cared about his employees and he believed that there was a possible future if they all cooperated and jointly thought about how they could reconsider the future. He likened the business to a snowball rolling downhill gathering more snow and momentum as it gained speed. He explained that there were two possible routes that this snowball could take. One possibility was for the snowball to grow in size and speed as it rolled downhill only to roll out onto the plain where it would melt and disappear. The other possibility was for the snowball to roll on down the mountain until it had become such a size and had such a speed that nothing could stop it until it reached the fertile valley at the bottom of the mountain. For him the fertile valley represented a revitalised business. 'We can influence the path that snowball takes,' he explained. They did.

More recently I was involved with a company whose directors talked in terms of:

- 'Being in the firing line.'

- 'Attacking the competition.'

- 'Aiming at the target.'

They described the workforce as the 'troops'. Employees in this company did not 'step out of line', nor did those with any entrepreneurial style stay very long. I even saw a slide headed, 'We will fight them on the beaches.' Fight whom, I wonder?

Changing culture

Individuals and companies have metaphors that express their unique culture. The question is whether or not it is a metaphor that supports the culture and style that they really want. The clue is in the language and the behaviour of the individuals, just as the language in the company described above highlighted the military metaphor that permeated everything that the managers said. Not surprisingly many of the older managers in this company had spent time in the forces. Now the company was searching for a way of developing a new style of leader who encouraged autonomy and cooperation. It was time to change the metaphor that underpinned the culture of this company.

Listen to the language that colleagues and friends use. Have you heard these sorts of statements:

'I need to *combat* his response.'
'We can *overcome* objections.'
'We need to *keep our heads down.*'

'On *track* to achieve what we want.'
'*Steaming* ahead.'
'We will carry no *passengers.*'

'Everything in the garden is *rosy.*'
'They are *blooming.*'
'Business has *died down.*'

When you are aware of the metaphor by which you, friends, colleagues live your lives you will be aware of the way you and they are thinking. Understanding the metaphor both in and behind the communication can help you make sense of an individual's experience. If you know someone who thinks in terms of overcoming objections, you may begin to understand any resistance they experience from their colleagues, staff and customers. Imagine how you would feel if someone were attempting to *overcome* your objections!

Metaphors are rich in their ability to enhance communication. Here are some examples of the visual metaphors drawn by course delegates to depict either the way they saw themselves now or the way they wanted to see themselves in the future.

Visual metaphors

These pictures provide a wealth of information, not only for the observers but also for the owners. Questions can reveal many implications of the metaphor that have sometimes been outside its owner's awareness.

When thinking about what metaphors are true for you, you may find that it is your unconscious mind that pops an image or a thought into your head. Your unconscious mind is the source of your real hopes and fears. The more you learn to acknowledge what your unconscious tells you, the more you will have access to this powerful resource. Major breakthroughs in thinking are believed to have come about through the power of metaphor. It is held that Einstein discovered the theory of relativity as he lay daydreaming, imagining himself riding a sunbeam.

Your unconscious mind

THE STRUCTURE OF METAPHOR

Excellent communicators and influencers use metaphor to capture and hold attention. With metaphors they weave a spell.

The present life of men on earth, O King, as compared with the whole length of time which is unknowable to us, seems to me to be like this: as if, when you are sitting at dinner with your chiefs and ministers in wintertime,... one of the sparrows from outside flew very quickly through the hall; as if it came in one door and soon went out through another. In that actual time it is indoors it is not touched by the winter's storm; but the tiny period of calm is over in a moment, and having come out of the winter it soon returns to the winter and slips out of your sight. Man's life appears to be more or less like this; and of what may follow it, or what preceded it, we are absolutely ignorant.

The Venerable Bede

Story metaphors

Metaphors can be useful when there is some opposition or conflict: they can't be argued with. They can be a valuable tool in business presentations when you want to avoid or overcome resistance. In such cases the metaphor could be a story you develop to make a point or it could be an incident from your own experience. The benefit of using an incident from your own experience in a presentation is that you are unlikely to need notes to recall it and it is indisputable.

A metaphor respects the power of the unconscious mind by allowing it to reach its own conclusions. A metaphor is like a puzzle — the unconscious mind tussles with it until a solution is reached that fits for you. The unconscious mind loves the challenge that the metaphor presents.

During my early NLP training with the UK Training School I always enjoyed the sessions given by David Gordon. David was a delightful storyteller and has written several books on the use of metaphor. At the end of one of these sessions he told us the story about the couple swimming to Japan that is included at the end of Chapter 2.2.

Unique interpretation

When I heard that story I tussled with it for days trying to make sense of it, until other thoughts took over. Occasionally it would come to mind but I still didn't make any real sense of it. Then two years later I was listening to a talk about goal setting and 'bingo', the whole point of the story fell into place. I really think the two-year wait helped me to appreciate it that much more than if I'd got it straight away. The metaphor made unique sense to me at the time and in the way that was right for me.

The fascinating thing about a complex metaphor is that it makes sense in different ways to different people. Your unconscious mind will work out a meaning that fits for you. A metaphor respects your ability to learn what you need from what it offers. This is why it is not the custom to explain the meaning of a metaphor.

The metaphor at the end of this section was created by one of our course delegates following the guidelines set out in Chapter 3.4, Write Your Own Metaphor. She created this metaphor for her 'buddie' on the course, her partner in personal development sessions. The metaphor was designed to help her partner achieve her desired personal outcomes. She had 15 minutes in which to write the metaphor. It was a creative, spontaneous process. Metaphors can be as enjoyable in the writing as in the giving and the receiving.

THE DOOR TO CREATIVITY

I recently had a meeting with a manager in the Mars corporation. I was impressed with the values and style they brought to the business. We were discussing the impact that Mars ice creams had on the ice cream market in general, how it had raised the quality of ice creams, not only of their own manufacture but of others' too.

The manager I was talking to worked for a division of the Mars corporation that sold ice cream to countries including Africa, India and the United Arab Emirates. One of the factors that influences the quality of the ice cream is the temperature at which it is kept. If this is too high then the quality of the ice cream deteriorates. In the UK there are strict controls on the conditions in which food produce must be kept, but this is not the case in some other countries. To guarantee the condition of the ice cream, Mars decided to provide those countries with freezers in which to keep the ice cream. The regulation temperature for ice cream in the UK is −18°C. The Mars freezers are set to keep the ice cream at a temperature of −25°C. The company owns these freezers and recognises that to ensure the quality of the product it must manage the product environment.

Coincidentally we were having problems with a hotel booked by one of our clients for a series of courses we were running for them. I applied the Mars thinking to the problems we were

Metaphorical thinking

experiencing. The Mars situation acted as a metaphor for my experience with the hotel: the freezer was the environment for the ice cream, just as the hotel is the environment for the training. To ensure the quality of the training we needed to ensure the quality of the hotel, especially in those we didn't personally select. The result of this has been that we now provide free training for the staff of the hotels in which we do the work. This is appreciated by the staff and of course helps to ensure the quality of the training: a win/win situation.

The point is that thinking metaphorically can generate many new and different ideas that will benefit your customers, your staff, your business and your life.

SUMMARY

Metaphors have been with us in many forms for as long as we can remember. Stories in the forms of fairy tales, proverbs and parables are passed down from generation to generation. Metaphors are so rooted in our upbringing that for many people they act as an anchor for relaxation and involvement. As such, metaphors bypass any conscious blocks or resistance and slip into the unconscious mind. The unconscious mind responds to the challenge of the metaphor by finding a unique solution that fits the listener's experience and needs.

Skilled communication

Metaphors are powerful and memorable. Many of the most memorable speakers and leaders use metaphor as a way of communicating what they want to say. A skilled story teller is a skilled communicator.

Metaphors are also used in our everyday lives. The metaphors in an individual's or company's language provide many clues to the patterns by which that individual lives their life and the culture of the company of which they are a part. By learning how to construct and recount metaphors you will be learning how to open your listener's or reader's mind to new possibilities and choices.

THOUGHT PROVOKERS

1   If you were to draw a metaphor for yourself, what would you draw? As you read that question you may have noticed that a picture popped into your mind. What was it?

●   What does this represent for you?

●   What are the characteristics of this metaphor?

●   What are its strengths?

●   What are its weaknesses?

●   How are the elements of the image connected?

●   What does this signify?

●   What is missing and what does that signify?

Show the drawing to someone else and encourage them to ask you questions about it. Their questions may give you insight into the deeper significance of the metaphor for you.

2   What metaphors would you use to describe:

●   your career?

●   your relationships?

●   your social life?

●   your past?

●   your future?

How do the characteristics of the metaphor manifest themselves in these areas of your life? For example, if you say, 'life is like a dream', what does that mean? Is it unreal? Dreams can be intangible. Dreams have many meanings and the purpose of them can be unclear. There are pleasant dreams and nightmares. Explore the possibilities of the metaphor for you.

3   Think of a situation that you would like to influence. It could be a presentation or a meeting or a discussion with one of your colleagues. Develop a metaphor that you can use the next time you are in this situation.

> 4   Think now of the company that you manage or work
>   for. Is there a metaphor that expresses itself through
>   the language and actions of the employees? Set
>   yourself the task of identifying any metaphors that
>   you hear being used in your company or in the
>   companies of any of your customers during a
>   particular day.

Many years ago there existed a village, tucked away in a remote part of the world. The village was in a deep valley surrounded by gentle green hills. The vegetation was rich and fertile and everyone who lived in the village had all the food and water they needed. The animals that belonged to the villagers roamed free and the children played happily in the warm sunshine.

One day, a strange beast crept over the top of the hill. The villagers had never seen such a weird creature before and they threw spears at the creature, to no avail. The creature stayed where it was until dusk when it sloped away into the dark.

Every day at dawn the beast would reappear and sit at the entrance to the valley. And every day at dusk it would return to the hills.

Over time the villagers grew used to the beast and they would feed it as they walked to work in the fields with their children. The children played happily in the fields, laughing and shouting. Gradually they approached the beast, and pushed and prodded it. The older villagers warned them to stop but they took no notice.

One day, a little girl threw a large rock at the beast, who howled in pain and turned and ran off to the hills. It did not return. The villagers became silent and sad and the little girl was upset.

Several years passed. The villagers had almost forgotten about the beast when it reappeared, bigger and older, lumbering over the hill and into the valley. The villagers were glad. When the little girl saw the beast again she ran up to it and kissed it. She knew exactly what she would do next ...

Programming

The process of coding talent is known as **modelling**. When you step into someone else's shoes and reproduce the way they do what they do and the results that they achieve, then you are modelling. Modelling involves reproducing the same sequence of thinking, language and behaviour patterns as your subject. To do this, you may also need to take on (albeit temporarily) their identity and beliefs. In effect, to use a computer metaphor, you are eliciting the program code needed to demonstrate the talent and you are running the program as and when you want it.

The purpose of modelling talent in business is to reproduce excellence. If you want to reproduce the success of an outstanding salesperson, manager or presenter, modelling enables you to do this. These top performers will run mental and physical programs of which they are unaware and which will almost certainly not be in any book on standard selling techniques, management models or presentation skills. The programs that they run may be specific to the industry, the client or even to the place and occasion. Excellence, as such, is context specific. You may discover that parts of their program add little or no value and yet other parts can be developed, resulting in an enhancement of the talent under study.

So in essence, NLP is an active process. The more you model excellence, the more you discover. NLP operates at a higher level than most traditional training. It offers ownership and discovery and enables you to learn how to learn.

Reproducing excellence

Learn how to learn

1.6 Modelling

Sitting by Nellie

If someone can do it, anyone can do it. That is the basis of modelling. Modelling is concerned more with the how than with the why. There is a joke which says that NLPers don't introduce themselves by saying 'How do you do?' but 'How do you do that?'

Modelling can take many forms. Some of your most fundamental skills will have been learned by modelling others. Babies and young children are expert modellers. Only when they start learning by more traditional methods do they begin to lose this skill. 'Sitting by Nellie' was the method by which many employees were taught to do their work. This only worked well if Nellie was a model of excellence or if the new employee was smart enough to know what worked and what didn't. Unfortunately, 'sitting by Nellie' often resulted in the reproduction of bad practice.

You can model anything — people are excellent in many different spheres. You can, for example, have excellence in the ability to:

- generate commitment and respect;

- motivate yourself and others;

- sell and influence;

- achieve a personal best in sport;

- listen;

- speak a language fluently;

and so on.

But equally you can have excellence in your ability to:

- get depressed;

- sulk;

- lose your temper;

- remain untouched by emotion;

- procrastinate;

- worry.

By modelling any of these you can develop a conscious awareness of the process, and with conscious awareness you have choice, choice to continue the same process or choice to do something else.

You can apply the process of modelling to yourself. You might, for example, want to reproduce an ability or skill that you have in some areas of your life or work, in order to use it in other contexts. Let's suppose you are influential when dealing with colleagues but don't have the same level of influence with clients. You could model yourself in order to discover the difference so that you can use your influence in whatever context you choose.

Transferring a skill

Many companies now have a system of mentoring whereby members of staff, as a part of their development, are allocated to a more senior or a more experienced employee in order to learn from them ('sitting by Nellie' relabelled!). All too often the success of this system hinges on the experienced employee's ability to impart the skills they have. Often they don't know their most powerful skills nor how they use them. If, however, the learner is equipped with the NLP modelling skills, then they can elicit the skills they need to learn. The subject being modelled can also benefit from this process by becoming aware of how they structure their experience. With this awareness they can more consistently reproduce the skills desired.

Mentoring

STRATEGIES

NLP is a way of coding excellence. We achieve the results we do through the programs we run. Just as computer programs are a sequence of codes, so personal programs are a sequence of mental and behavioural codes. When you walk, talk, drive, read, laugh, it is unlikely that you think consciously about how you do these things. The programs that make them happen are managed on your behalf by your unconscious mind. These programs are known as strategies.

Unconscious strategies

Nevertheless, if you want to model excellence either in yourself or in other people, your aim is to elicit these unconscious strategies as well as the conscious strategies that enable you to do what you do. When you have the strategy for how someone managed their experience, you have the key to reproducing that experience for yourself.

When a chef produces a gourmet dinner, not only is he following a recipe for the ingredients, he is also following a recipe for thinking and behaviour. He may, for example, have an image of what he wants the dish to look like accompanied by the aroma of the final meal. He may also be concerned with timings and the look and feel of the ingredients. He has a unique way of achieving the result.

Decision-making strategies

You have strategies for making decisions such as what to have for dinner, where to go on holiday, how to plan your day. There will be a pattern to the way you do this.

For example, the way I decided to write this book was:

1   I saw others (close friends) write a book.

2   I imagined myself writing a book.

3   I asked myself repeated questions over time about what the topic would be and how I would do it.

4   I looked and listened for examples of how others did this.

5   I committed myself by telling people what I planned to do.

Understanding a strategy gives me choice about how and when I use it. Equally if someone wanted to influence my decision about writing it would help if they understood my strategy rather than trying to impose their own.

Suppose you identify that your partner in negotiation has a

strategy for negotiation that involves:

1   Creating a picture of what they want (visual).

2   Asking themselves a question about the viability of
     that outcome (auditory).

3   Getting a feeling of certainty that this is what they
     want (feelings).

By matching this strategy you will be helping and influencing
their decision-making process. Let's say their outcome was to
ask for promotion to a new job. You could match their strategy
by saying:

1   'Imagine what it would be like to approach your boss,
     to see yourself with her clarifying your future' (visual).

2   'Ask yourself if that is a feasible thing to do'
     (auditory).

3   'And you will instinctively know whether this is the
     right approach for you' (feelings).

Matching strategies

It is important to remember that if you ask someone 'How do
you do that?', i.e. if you ask them to consciously recall their
strategy, it is unlikely that they will be able to give it to you.
They may either say 'I don't know', or they will tell you what
they think they do. This is rarely the same as what they actually
do. To elicit a strategy, the person you are modelling needs to
be doing or reliving the experience that you wish to model.
    To find out more about how to model a skill, see Chapter 3.5
in the Toolkit.

MODELLING IN BUSINESS

Modelling in business has led to significant breakthroughs in
the way that skills are taught.
    Traditionally, companies have used standard training
programmes to teach standard skills. More often than not,
trainees were left to their own devices to adapt these skills to
their unique environment. There are unique patterns that work
in one company, one department, one market segment and
that will not work in another. Modelling enables you to elicit
these context specific patterns in order to reproduce
excellence in your own unique environment. By choosing the

Consistency in performance

people who excel within your organisation, not only will you be able to reproduce their levels of success but you will also be able to help your models of excellence achieve a greater consistency in their own performance.

The modelling process involves observing and listening to the exemplars in action in the relevant context to identify what they do and how they do it. Your sensitivity, flexibility and ability to build rapport are crucial in this process. When interviewing your subject, watch and listen carefully rather than relying on what your subject tells you. Their eye movements, their use of language and the subtle changes in their non-verbal behaviour carry a wealth of information.

Refining the strategy

The joy of modelling is that you can refine the model by testing which elements add to the excellence and which detract or make no difference. By taking away one element at a time you can determine how this affects the overall result. This enables you to generate the most effective model, which you can use to teach others, even the subject themselves.

This process applies when modelling anything, whether it be an individual or a team or a complete organisation. The skills it takes to sell a luxury car are quite different from the skills it takes to sell a software package. The skill required to motivate a group of production line workers is quite different from the skill needed to motivate advertising account executives. Modelling enables you to uncover the uniqueness of the model, the quality of the inborn talent and the natural skill.

A BENCHMARK FOR EXCELLENCE

The result of much of the modelling that has taken place has been the discovery of certain patterns of excellence. I offer this benchmark for excellence with caution. It is not fixed, it continues to develop. I offer it as a short cut to excellence today, but tomorrow...?

THE ELEMENTS OF EXCELLENCE

I use the term excellence to mean individuals and organisations who consistently achieve the goals they set themselves. People and organisations who achieve excellence:

Systems

- pay attention to how they fit into the larger system of which they are a part. Their mission is designed to add value to the larger system; it is ecological in its nature. Anita Roddick, founder of The Body Shop, seeks to enhance the countries with which she trades. Also increasingly successful are travel companies who respect the culture of the countries to which they travel. The exploitative development of such places as the Costa Brava was replaced by a more environmentally sensitive management as tourism declined. Only now that people are beginning to put back what was once stripped away has interest in these areas resurfaced.

- have a commonly held and understood mission or identity. If it is a team or an organisation this mission will be an expression of what each respective team or company member really wants. So often companies have mission statements on the wall which the employees cannot even remember.

    Companies whose only motive is profit have faced increasing difficulties and many have disappeared. The same is true for individuals and teams. What value do they or you add to the system of which you are a part? Managers whose only contribution to the system is interference and delay are tolerated less and less.

Mission

- hold and live out beliefs of excellence. They believe that:

Beliefs

— each person is unique;

— everyone makes the best choice available to them at the time they make it;

— there is no failure, only feedback;

— behind all behaviour is a positive intention;

— the meaning of the communication is its effect;

— there is a solution to every problem;

— the person with the most flexibility in thinking and behaviour has the best chance of succeeding;

— mind and body are part of the same system;

— knowledge, thought, memory and imagination are the result of sequences and combinations of ways of filtering and storing information.

These beliefs are explained in detail in Chapter 2.1.

Capabilities

● are capable of:

— sensitivity towards themselves and others. They are able to recognise changes in their own and others' states and respond to those changes.

— flexibility in being able to change what they are doing and how they are doing it when what they are doing isn't working. As a comparison, for years people in some market sectors have been taught a specific sales procedure — 10 steps to selling double glazing, insurance, a car. Probably even worse are some of the salespeople who don't use any steps at all. How different it is when you are dealing with someone who employs both sensitivity and flexibility in the way they approach and respond to you.

— thinking in outcome terms and the ability to integrate their and your outcome into one. This technique is referred to as **dovetailing** by Genie Laborde in her beautiful book *Influencing with Integrity*.

Behaviour

● act and speak on a day by day basis that lives out their mission, their beliefs and their capabilities. By watching and listening to them it is evident what their mission, beliefs and capabilities are. Their behaviour is congruent, consistent, free of mixed messages. They operate on a set of principles that form the basis of everything they do.

Environment

● recognise that their environment is an expression of who they are and what they think. They choose people and places who share the same values, have common outcomes and who are engaged in the learning process.

The application of NLP grows every day. It has been used to find out how famous leaders generate commitment and passion. We have used NLP to find out how they think, how they use language and what subtle changes in their body language influence the response they receive. We have studied skilled negotiators, people who can discuss the most sensitive of issues and lead the discussion to an agreement that gains the commitment of all involved.

Sport has given a lot to business thinking in recent years. An understanding of how top athletes excel enables us to grasp the components of self-motivation and take those principles for ourselves.

There are many, many more examples. Salespeople who can relate to their customers' unexpressed needs, presenters who can put over information in a compelling, motivating way, consultants who by the most elegant of questions can trigger off profound change. How do they do it? NLP is providing the answers.

SUMMARY

NLP is the process of modelling. The skills and techniques explained in the later chapters of this book are the result of modelling excellence. As such it is an ever changing, ever growing subject. When you engage in NLP you engage in a powerful learning process that is constantly developing. This is what continuous improvement is all about.

Continuous improvements

The result of modelling is conscious competence, a mastery of the skills you have and the skills you want to have. Subsequently it becomes unconscious competence. It becomes a natural part of who you are. In its simplest form it is a process you have been using all of your life. In its most sophisticated form it is a way of generating excellence in everything that you do, as an individual, as a team, as a company.

Some people have shied away from NLP because of the passion with which others have proclaimed its benefits. Nevertheless some of the concerns about this enthusiasm and zeal are to do with the power of the technique. It works. It does indeed make a difference.

THOUGHT PROVOKERS
I In what unique ways do you add value to: ● your family?   ● your role in your business?   ● your friendships?   ● the community of which you are a part?   ● life?

2   Think about the events you have planned for the rest
    of this week. Are there any about which you don't feel
    too confident or happy? Think of someone you know
    who could handle these events in the way that you
    would like to. Step into their shoes and imagine
    yourself handling these events as if you were that
    other person.

3   Who have been the main influences on the way you
    are today? What is it about each that you have
    incorporated into the person you are?

4   Who would you most like to resemble in skill or in
    style? Is there a colleague or a friend whose style and
    skill you admire? Imagine how you might come to
    resemble them.

One day a man was tending his garden which bordered on the desert in
Arizona. Dusk was descending and he heard in the distance the sound of
motorbikes. A gang of Hell's Angels rode up, attacked him, tied him to
the back of one of the bikes and drove him into the desert. There they left
him barely alive as night fell. The man survived the night and began to
regain consciousness as the sun appeared above the horizon.

He knew that the sun in the desert means certain death. Without
food, water or shelter he stood no chance of survival. Then at his side he
noticed a small bush. He crawled underneath and curled up using the
little shade there was to protect himself from the burning rays of the sun.
He felt despair — no one knew where he was.

Just at that moment he saw a falcon landing on the branch of the
bush. To the man's amazement the falcon spoke and asked, 'Can I help
you?'

Shocked, the man replied, 'I am dying of thirst, my mouth and
tongue are swollen. To survive I need water.'

'Look behind you,' said the falcon. 'There is a snake. Follow the
snake, for it knows where the water seeps out of the rocks. There you will
be able to drink.'

The man returned to the bush, and the next day the falcon came
back. 'How are you?' the falcon asked.

'I have drunk but I need food to survive — water alone is not enough.'

'Stay quiet and wait until the antelope passes by. When it does, follow
it — it can show you where the cactus plants are whose flesh you can
eat.'

Sure enough, when the man followed the antelope he found food and was able to eat. Feeling fitter he returned to the bush and once again the falcon arrived. 'Can I do anything for you?'

'Yes,' replied the man. 'Although I have drunk and eaten I still need salt to survive. How can I get the salt I need to live?'

'Have no fear,' said the falcon. 'The fox also needs salt. If you follow the fox you will see where it finds the rocks to lick that will give you the salt you need.'

The man did as the falcon said and the next day returned to find that the bush under which he had sheltered was burned and charred. 'What will I do now?' asked the man. 'I have no shelter, I will burn to death.'

Then the man realised he had been out in the desert each day following the animals. He had learned how to find food, water and salt. He knew how to survive. He noticed the rich colours of the sky as the sun dipped low on the horizon, the blues, the purples and the gold of the sun itself. He heard the exquisite songs of the birds in the distance and he felt an inner peace and joy.

'Shall I show you the way home?' asked the falcon.

The man thought for a moment and then said, 'I think I'll stay a little longer.'

PART 2

MANAGING

WITH NLP

Once you have explored the elements of NLP, the exciting part is putting those skills together in many different ways to achieve the results you want. One of the principles of the way that NLP is taught is that it starts with yourself.

A woman took her son to see Gandhi who asked what she wanted. 'I'd like you to get him to stop eating sugar,' she replied.

'Bring the boy back in two weeks' time,' replied Gandhi.

Two weeks later the woman returned with her son. Gandhi turned to the boy and said, 'Stop eating sugar.'

The woman looked surprised and asked, 'Why did I have to wait two weeks for you to say that?'

'Two weeks ago I was eating sugar,' Gandhi replied.

Example as influence

By first learning to manage yourself with NLP you will become a model of the principles that will influence those around you. For example, once you have learned how NLP can help you to set compelling goals for yourself, you will be more able to facilitate the setting of compelling goals for others.

'Example is not the main thing in influencing others. It is the only thing.'
Albert Schweitzer

By using NLP to manage yourself you will be influencing those around you through your example more than through your words. Your actions teach to the unconscious mind.

The techniques covered in this section of the book require you to have read about the elements of NLP. These techniques bring together these elements and have been discovered through the process of modelling excellence. They are not techniques dreamed up by trainers or consultants, they are those used by people who achieve excellence, ones that work for them and that will work for you.

What works

In modelling excellence some common threads began to emerge: the difference that makes the difference. By learning to use these techniques you will be learning how to achieve the results that you want in a way that dovetails with the needs and desires of those around you. For many people the result of applying these techniques is the achievement of personal congruence, a sense of being true to yourself in a way that enables you to achieve your full potential. NLP has the power to help you continually to develop that potential to keep on developing and learning in ways that efficiently harness your energy.

The topics included in this part of the book are as follows.

The beliefs of excellence, Chapter 2.1. These are a set of beliefs that have emerged as common themes for those people who achieve personal congruence. Many management teams are exploring the areas of mission, vision, beliefs and values as a way of providing direction for their companies. The resultant statements can often appear flat and lifeless when they are not supported by the day to day behaviour of the managers and employees. This section shows you how to step into these beliefs of excellence in a way that brings them to life.

Chapter 2.2 covers **outcome thinking**. The process of modelling people who are able consistently to achieve their goals has uncovered the characteristics of what are called well formed outcomes.

It is interesting to contrast the elements of this approach with some of the standard objective-setting approaches that are used in business. The difference between the NLP approach and many of the techniques that have been taught previously is that NLP provides us with the tools to find out what *really* makes the difference. How often have you learned techniques on training programmes only to return to work and resume your normal practices after a day or two? If the techniques worked then you would probably continue to use them. If you apply all the elements of outcome thinking, as with all other NLP techniques, then you will begin to experience an increase in the incidence of you achieving what you want.

One of the most important skills discovered in people who were models of excellence was their ability to influence and bring about change in ways that were effective by being both powerful and fast. As well as using techniques to achieve these results it was also discovered that there was one common element in all their approaches: their ability to build almost immediate **rapport** with the people with whom they were working. I would go so far as to say that I believe that this is one of the most important skills in business today. Without rapport few management systems will work. With rapport you will generate cooperation, commitment and respect. Chapter 2.3 will teach you how to build and maintain rapport with the people with whom you come into contact. When using any of the other skills of NLP it is crucial that you ensure that you have and maintain rapport.

All the elements of NLP complement each other. Each adds another piece to the jigsaw of excellence. A more recent development in NLP thinking is that of **perceptual positions**, explained in Chapter 2.4. This approach complements outcome thinking especially, as it is a way of taking a balanced approach to situations and outcomes. Those people who are most able to find a solution or a way forward that fits with the other people involved have the ability to appreciate situations from different positions. Whereas some of the NLP techniques involve paying attention to the details of thinking and behaviour, the perceptual positions technique provides a powerful short cut to achieving the same results.

Many of the NLP techniques are concerned with how to manage your thinking process and how to manage yourself so that you can utilise your talents and resources to the full. **Anchoring**, Chapter 2.5, is an approach for enabling you to access your personal resources when you want them by making connections between these resources and something that works as a trigger for you. The use of a specific trigger will then allow you to tap into the precise resource you want, when you want it. NLP operates on the principle that you already have all the resources you will ever need. Anchoring is the means by which you can utilise these resources to achieve your full potential.

Finally, Chapter 2.6 deals with the **logical levels of change**. These offer a model for identifying the level at which to intervene to bring about change for an individual, a team or an organisation. Meaningful and lasting change only occurs if it is thought through at all levels of environment, behaviour, capabilities and skills, beliefs and values, identity and mission. By thinking through change at each of these levels, you can generate an aligned state where every part of you is working towards the same outcome. This is the recipe for success and for achieving what you want.

2.1 Write Your Own Lifescript — Beliefs of Excellence

Stepping into beliefs

Your beliefs influence and mould your behaviour. They form your lifescript. In order to reproduce excellent performance it is necessary to be able to 'step into' the belief system held by the person you are modelling. 'Stepping into' someone else's belief system means that you presuppose that the other person's views are valid for as long as you want to reproduce the results of your model of excellence. To reproduce excellence in a congruent way it is necessary to model the identity, the beliefs, the values, the capabilities as well as the behaviour and the environment of your subject.

Modelling people who are excellent in what they do and who consistently achieve what they want led to the emergence of the following set of beliefs:

- Each person is unique.

- Everyone makes the best choice available to them at the time.

- There is no failure, only feedback.

- Behind every behaviour is a positive intention.

- The meaning of the communication is its effect.

- There is a solution to every problem.

- The person with the most flexibility in thinking and behaviour has the best chance of succeeding.

- Mind and body are part of the same system.

- Knowledge, thought, memory and imagination are the result of sequences and combinations of ways of filtering and storing information.

When modelling excellence you don't have to hold these as beliefs yourself, but if you presuppose them to be true you will be stepping into the hearts and minds of the people who do believe them. In so doing you begin to take on the ways of thinking and behaving that are characteristic of the models of excellence. This section explores these beliefs and how they manifest themselves in your everyday behaviour. But first let's explore how beliefs affect your experience.

HOW BELIEFS ORIGINATE

Jane was a newly appointed manager of a high class London store. The items for sale consisted of jewellery and expensive leather goods and were displayed in glass cabinets. Closing time was 6 o'clock. On the dot of 6 o'clock one of Jane's staff, Robert, would start locking the cabinets whether or not there were customers still in the store. Jane disapproved: she believed this gave the wrong impression to the customers. She wanted Robert to wait until all customers had left the store before locking the cabinets.

Although she explained to him that it was store policy to lock the cabinets only when customers had left, it had no effect. The next time it happened she pointed out that senior management disapproved of any locking up in the presence of customers; still no effect. Jane began to feel that she did not communicate any authority and was not getting the respect of her staff, particularly Robert.

In discussion with a friend she realised that what she should have said was, 'I want you to keep the cabinets open until all the customers have left.' She hadn't spoken for herself. She realised that by doing that she could begin to establish her own authority and power. And of course there were many other situations where she realised that she could begin to express what she herself wanted by saying 'I want' or 'I'd like'.

She wondered why she hadn't done this before and she came to realise that 'I want' was something she very rarely said. Then she remembered her childhood. Her mother had repeatedly said to her, 'I wants don't get', whenever she had said 'I want ...'

This is an example of how beliefs are formed. Opinions become facts. They aren't facts at all. They are perceptions formed by experience and the views of others.

Beliefs are views

Beliefs are views about yourself, others and the world that determine the decisions you take and the way you behave in everyday situations. Your parents or the equivalent of parent figures (and this includes teachers) will be the source of many of your beliefs.

For example:

- 'I want, doesn't get.'

- 'You always get what you want and you always will.'

- 'You'll always land on your feet whatever happens.'

- 'You're lazy.'

- 'You'll never get what you want in this world if you don't work for it.'

- 'You're an A grade pupil.'

- 'You're stupid.'

- 'People can't be trusted.'

- 'Children should be seen and not heard.'

- 'You've got no respect for anyone's feelings.'

- 'You're a liar.'

- 'You are the "good" child in the family.'

- 'You're a born artist.'

- 'You're a lousy mathematician.'

The magic of NLP is that you can change your beliefs so that you build your own set of beliefs to support the way you want to be. You need not carry around redundant or even destructive belief systems that belong to someone else. You can create your own empowering set of beliefs instead.

Rewrite history

There are several ways to do this. One way is to presuppose that you *do* hold beliefs that, although new to you, are more in line with the way you want to be. That is what this section is all about. Alternatively NLP gives you the techniques to rewrite your own history. Because your unconscious mind does not know the difference between what is real and what is imagined, you can imagine the past you would prefer to have had and rewrite your memories. The mental agility needed to do this comes as a result of learning the core skills of NLP, especially the thinking patterns explained in Chapter 1.1.

HOW BELIEFS INFLUENCE YOUR LIFE

My husband plays squash and he believes that he has the potential to win every match he plays. So what happens is that the sequence of events for him is as follows:

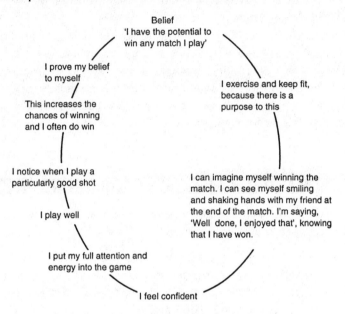

Enabling beliefs

If, on the other hand, he believed he did not have much chance of winning or playing well, this would be the scenario.

Limiting beliefs

Self-fulfilling prophecies

In this way your beliefs act as a self-fulfilling prophecy. You act in a way that proves the validity and value of your beliefs to yourself. Therefore, if your beliefs are self-limiting you will limit your performance, thus proving your belief to be true. Over time the beliefs become more and more entrenched as you continue to live them out each day.

However, if you hold empowering beliefs such as the beliefs of excellence, you will be acting and behaving in a way that releases your potential and allows you to express the real you. NLP gives you the key to generate empowering beliefs for yourself so that you can learn and grow and achieve the things you really want for yourself.

THE BELIEFS OF EXCELLENCE

Have you ever wondered how some people achieved the successes they did? For example:

- how Christopher Columbus held onto his vision of discovering a new route around the world and maintained the courage and tenacity to cross waters that no one had sailed before?

- how the Americans managed to break through the limits of what seemed possible, to land a man on the moon?

- how British hostage Terry Waite held onto his sanity and self-worth when held in solitary confinement bound, blindfolded and threatened with death?

- how Richard Branson carved out a share in the airline market for Virgin Airlines when the business was already dominated by well established and powerful companies?

Many people would have given up after a fraction of the journey. So what made these and so many more achievements possible? These people succeeded because they believed they could. Once Roger Bannister had run a mile in under four minutes, many other athletes did the same. Once he had broken the barrier, others knew it was possible.

EACH PERSON IS UNIQUE

This belief is sometimes referred to as 'The map is not the territory'.

Consider this conversation:

'I really enjoyed the film last night.'
'It was rubbish.'
'No it wasn't — the photography was beautiful.'
'Yes, but the story line was non-existent.'
'That's ridiculous.'
'No it isn't!'

Recognise that? Neither person in this conversation is right or wrong, although they may not appreciate this! However, each has their own way of experiencing life, their own 'map of the world'. How often does your 'map of the world' bump up against someone else's? And what happens when it does?

Once you accept that we do each have a unique map of the world then you begin to understand and accept difference.

Maps of the world

Imagine a world where this understanding and acceptance existed — how different our daily lives would be. How would the press survive? What stories would they print? Can you imagine how different the headlines would be?

How often are you party to the following kinds of situations?

Jim was explaining how he saw his future and the sort of obstacles he wanted to overcome. Jane listened to him for a while and then said, 'You know Jim, what you really ought to do is to leave this job and move into sales, you'd be much more suited to that.'

'But that isn't really what I want to do, Jane.'

'You may not think it is,' replied Jane, 'but believe me I know it's the right move for you.'

Jim sat back and folded his arms. He disagreed.

* * *

Diane could not understand why the staff in the company were complaining about the new appraisal scheme. She had been a member of the Personnel team who had been involved in its design. This involved managers rating their team members on a scale 1–5; 1 being 'subject to disciplinary action' and 5 meaning, more or less, that 'sun shines out of their eyes'. The staff were very unhappy about the form, particularly the rating system. Diane found all these complaints very frustrating and considered the staff to be 'difficult'.

Both of these illustrate what can happen when someone doesn't presuppose 'Each person is unique' to be true. So what does this mean? It means we all have our unique perception of

Perception

the world, the way things are, the way people behave, our own experience. And that perception is just a view of those things, an interpretation. It's not an exact representation of reality. So just like a map is only a representation of a territory, highlighting some features, ignoring others, so your personal experience leads you to highlight some features and ignore others.

Accepting this presupposition means that you respect difference.

Let's compare what it would be like to hold the belief that each person is unique with what it would be like not to do so.

	People who do believe that 'each person is unique' is true	People who don't believe that 'each person is unique' is true
Have this sort of approach	Cooperative, respectful and and open to difference	Rigid, inflexible and dogmatic
Hold these sorts of beliefs	That difference is valuable	That their opinion is right. They know best
Have these capabilities/ limitations	Listening skills, sensitivity to and respect for difference	Determination and single-mindedness
Do and say	Look interested, cooperate, ask questions, are curious about others' experiences and explore differences. Accept difference	Speak in terms of what others 'should' or 'ought' to do. Disagree and and interrupt. Dismiss
Feel	Relaxed and curious	Frustrated, irritated and stressed

EVERYONE MAKES THE BEST CHOICE AVAILABLE TO THEM AT THE TIME

When your colleague argues with you and refuses to see your point of view, *at that moment* it is the best choice available to them.

If you had learned the most elegant and cooperative ways of achieving what you want, life would be very different. But you didn't. You learned healthy and unhealthy ways of getting what you want. When a child cries and shouts in the middle of the supermarket, that child has learned that is the way to get the attention they want; not the best way, at least not for those around, but the best choice for the child. You do what you do because at some level it works, otherwise you wouldn't do it.

However, one thing is for sure:

If you do what you always did you get what you always got.

Consider for a moment one of your goals. What are you doing now to achieve it? Whatever that is, it is your best choice at this moment. The more choices you have the more chance you have of getting what you want. If one of your chosen paths doesn't get you what you want, you can choose another and another until you find the one that does.

New choices

List for a moment those people with whom you have felt frustrated within the last month. For example:

● the manager who gave a boring presentation;

● the colleague who dominated the meeting;

● a member of your family who didn't do as you expected;

● the car driver who cut in front of you;

● the salesperson who wouldn't answer your questions;

● the receptionist who kept you waiting.

Now step into the belief that 'everyone makes the best choice available to them at the time'.

Imagine what it would be like if you were to believe that. It doesn't matter if you actually don't. Now, as you imagine what it is like, how does that affect your feelings towards these people you have listed? Would that manager really have chosen to have given a boring presentation if he had had a choice? Would the colleague have dominated the meeting if they had had other choices about how to influence you?

This may not be your belief, but you can experience the results of holding it by *presupposing* that it is true for you.

If you don't hold this to be true you might respond to the deliverer of the boring presentation with disdain. By presupposing that this is their best choice, you might be more

Choosing responses

likely to give them constructive feedback and suggestions for other ways they could present their ideas.

The focus shifts from being one of blame, disdain and frustration to being one of curiosity, understanding and concern, particularly in terms of how to enable others around you and yourself to have more choice, so that the 'best choice' for one or a few becomes the 'best choice' for many.

How many people do you know who live their life with regrets? Do you? Knowing what you know now there may very well be decisions you would change, places you would have gone, people you would have treated differently. But this is you now, with different skills, different knowledge, different experience. At that time the choices you made were the *best* available to you. Once you can accept this you can let go of regrets; they clutter the places reserved for more choices.

THERE IS NO FAILURE, ONLY FEEDBACK

Christopher Columbus, John F Kennedy, Terry Waite, Richard Branson, Roger Bannister are all people who persevered to get what they wanted against all odds, people who held the belief that 'There is no failure, only feedback'. I'm sure if we interviewed Christopher Columbus today that he would not say, 'Well actually, I put it all down to this belief, "no failure only feedback"'! There is no doubt, however, that this must have been how he viewed his experience in order to give himself the courage and tenacity to carry on with his explorations and the desire to discover new routes around the world.

Recipe for learning

Experience and acceptance of failure = defeat
and resignation
Experience and review of feedback = learning
and choice

Imagine that you hold this belief to be true. How would it influence how you respond to:

● your acceptance of feedback from others?

● your confidence in giving feedback?

● your self-esteem when presenting ideas?

● your willingness to take risks?

Try it on for size — what would it really be like for you? Imagine the learning potential this can unleash.

Wow! This belief can be mind-blowing. It means that behind every action is a positive intention towards you. The key thing to remember here is that it doesn't have to be true. The benefits come from believing that it is true. This affects the choices you have in the way you respond. However, those people who are able to maintain choices in the way they respond to the behaviour of those around them believe this to be true.

Ian and his teenage son had almost come to blows. His son stood in one corner of the kitchen and Ian in the other. They shouted but neither listened to the other. To Ian his son was being a demanding, inconsiderate teenager. To the son his father had a closed mind, was inflexible and completely out of touch. Ian stopped himself from rushing forward and hitting his son and in that moment he gave himself the time to stand back and think about what he was doing. He moved towards his son, put his arms around him and said, 'I'll always love you, no matter what you do.'

That moment enabled Ian to express what he really felt. That moment would also imprint itself on his son's mind in such a way that when he had a teenage son of his own he had this memory, this role model of how a father can be.

Now at that point Ian was not consciously thinking, 'What is the positive intention behind my son's behaviour towards me?' But at some level, a more unconscious level, this is the principle that was in operation. It certainly wasn't in his son's mind to think, 'How can I be so disagreeable that I cause my Dad to give me a role model of parenting for my future?' — far from it! But by acting as if this were the case Ian turned what might have been a damaging situation into a special one. This is the sort of influence you can have. If you choose to believe that there is a positive intention towards you in the following kinds of circumstances you can transform the way you respond to the situation. For example:

A boss shouts at you, blaming you for incompetence	You could choose to believe that the positive intention towards you is to provide you with the opportunity to learn how to stay calm and confident when faced with aggression

BEHIND EVERY BEHAVIOUR IS A POSITIVE INTENTION

Acting 'as if'

| A colleague misunderstands what you tell him or her | The positive intention is to teach you how to be more flexible in your communication so that you find a way of explaining which they do understand |

These examples may or may not work for you. It is important to generate your own ideas of what the positive intentions might be, ones that make sense of the behaviour for you. This is an opportunity to let your creativity generate some ideas for you. You will know when you have identified a positive intention towards you that fits. It will give the behaviour a whole new meaning. More than that, it will free you from giving a compulsive response: it will change your state so that your response is one made out of choice.

THE MEANING OF THE COMMUNICATION IS ITS EFFECT

This can also be expressed as 'the intention behind a communication is not its meaning'. The principle operates at many different levels.

Have you ever experienced a moment of frustration when you have carefully explained an idea to someone and they have misunderstood you? Or have you ever given feedback to someone with the intention of helping them to learn and develop, only to find that they felt angry about what you had said?

At parents' evenings at school, sometimes I shuddered when a teacher said things like, 'this particular class are a difficult group to teach, they aren't good listeners. They've got to learn to pay attention.' I wonder who the teacher thinks is responsible for helping them to pay attention.

How often have you been involved in a performance appraisal when you had the impression that your standard of performance had nothing whatsoever to do with your manager who was appraising you? How did you feel?

If you have a team working for you and they are achieving results beyond the norm, that is a measure of your management ability.

If you have a colleague who won't cooperate with you, that is a reflection of your influencing skill.

If you have a child who won't 'behave' that is a statement about your ability as a parent.

The other people in these situations have a part too! But you are a part of the system. Something you do is allowing and possibly even encouraging the response you receive.

The power in this way of thinking is that it gives you responsibility for and ownership of the responses you receive. This means that you will then do something about it if you don't get the response you want. For example, if someone doesn't understand you, you will find a way of explaining your thoughts so that they do.

Your environment and experience are an expression of who you are.

John, a manager, came to me for advice on a problem he had with a member of his staff. John managed a team of systems designers who generally were a quiet group and worked independently. In the type of work they did there wasn't much need for them to talk to each other. They typically worked on separate projects at their individual workstations. Dave, however, liked to talk and would engage anyone around him in conversation to such an extent that he seriously affected the progress of the work in the department.

John had mentioned this to Dave several times and asked him not to interrupt the others working, with little effect. In desperation, John told the other members of the department not to speak to Dave except at coffee and lunchtime. The result of this was that he was now getting complaints from other managers who said that Dave was wandering into their departments, talking to their staff and interrupting the work.

I asked John what he had done as a result of this. He said, 'I brought Dave into my office, sat him down and talked to him for ages about the problems he was causing.' Needless to say this hadn't resolved the problem. On the contrary, Dave must have been inwardly delighted. What a way to get the undivided attention of his manager, someone to talk to legitimately!

Once John recognised that the meaning of his communication was the response from Dave he had other choices. Rather than aggravating the situation by denying Dave conversation, he started to plan ways in which Dave could usefully contribute to discussions and meetings with other departments. The result was that Dave's role and style became an asset to the department. Not only that but Dave really enjoyed his new role, his needs were satisfied. A 'win' for everyone.

The meaning of your communication is its effect means that:

If you have people working for you who give their all to their work	It is an indication of how you manage them

Responsibility

If you explain a new concept to a colleague and they don't understand	It is a measure of your explanation
If you have a warm loving family around you	It is a reflection of how you are
If you give feedback to a friend and they are offended	It is a result of how you gave the feedback

Flexibility

Anyone holding the belief that 'the meaning of your communication is the effect' does not have problem customers, problem staff, problem management. Holding this belief means you take responsibility and ownership for the reactions you get and you act on these reactions. By holding this belief you do not consider others to be a source of problems. You seek to develop your own flexibility so that you find new choices that elicit new responses.

THERE IS A SOLUTION TO EVERY PROBLEM

What do you do when you are faced with a problem? Do you give up? Do you persevere until you find a way out? Do you wait for someone else to sort it out?

Imagine what it would be like to believe that you could find a solution to every problem you ever encountered in life. Worry would fly out of the window, you could rest assured that there will always be a way forward.

That is what it is like to hold this belief. This is the belief of people in history who have made the major breakthroughs. People who find the new solutions to old problems. They do this because they believe they can. This is the belief at the heart of all creativity.

Edward de Bono explores the consequences of this belief in his books about lateral thinking. There is a solution to every problem and believing this opens the mind to the possibilities, new, zany, innovative solutions.

If you hold this belief you are more likely to trust your instinct to find a way forward.

THE PERSON WITH THE MOST FLEXIBILITY IN THINKING AND BEHAVIOUR HAS THE BEST CHANCE OF SUCCEEDING

At one stage in my career I worked for the training department of a large computer manufacturer. We ran a variety of skills development courses for the customers of this company. At that time I was involved in an influencing skills course which gave the delegates a greater command and choice in the way they expressed themselves verbally. We also taught them how to choose the most effective language to achieve the outcomes they wanted, particularly for meetings. So we sent back to the clients some highly verbally skilled people. Then we started to get complaints from the company sales teams. When a company sales person was in a meeting with a client who had attended the influencing skills course, the company person was consistently being outshone by the client in the way they managed the meeting. Needless to say the company changed its training policy at that point. This course immediately became a key part of the training programme for the sales teams!

* * *

On holiday this year I began to enjoy playing badminton and felt pleased with my ability to play close to the net and return the low shots. However, if my co-player lobbed the shuttle high over my head forcing me to turn back I often missed or hit the shuttlecock into the net.

A skilled player is one who can approach the net and make the low returns, one who can run backwards and catch the high lobs, one who can tip the shuttlecock gently over the net and who has the mastery to be able to place the shuttlecock in any part of the opponent's court that they choose. Flexibility is the key to success.

If you have flexibility in your thinking and your behaviour you have choices available to you. If one choice doesn't work you can try another until you find one that does. So how does a sports player get flexibility? They train, they exercise the different parts of their body so that they can move freely, so that they can vary their style. The variety of the training programmes that athletes undergo is extensive. The most effective exercise is often the simplest but most frequent. By regularly practising the skills and techniques explained in this book you will develop your range of behaviour and thinking and consequently your flexibility.

Exercise your thinking

Anything that occurs in one part of the system will affect the other parts.

MIND AND BODY ARE PART OF THE SAME SYSTEM

Stand up to do the following exercise. Look ahead, stand feet apart, face forward, raise one arm horizontally out in front of you and gently twist around, keeping your arm horizontal until your arm is pointing as far behind you as it will go. Keeping your arm fixed in that position, turn round and note what your arm is pointing to. It may be a point on the wall or in the distance that marks how far you have been able to move your arm behind you.

Now look carefully at the scene behind you and decide how far you would like your arm to be able to move beyond the original point. Fix that point in your mind as you turn to face forward again. As you face forward twist again, moving your arm behind you as far as it will go. When you have pushed it as far as it will go, hold it steady, turn round and see how far you have moved your arm this time.

The power of the mind

Most people find that they have moved their arm further the second time; if not to the point they visualised, then beyond. We know that if you imagine yourself throwing a ball, for example, the muscles of the body that would move if you were actually throwing a ball do tense and flex in exactly the same way.

Those of you with a vivid imagination probably recoil physically when watching something unpleasant on TV or the cinema. You can reproduce the feelings in yourself that are experienced by someone else. Your body becomes an expression of your thinking. Recent research has shown many connections between what we think and the well-being of our bodies.

The point about all these beliefs of excellence is that *they don't have to be true*. Their power lies in the effect they have when you choose to believe they are true. So what are the implications for you of believing that mind and body are part of the same system?

- You would be independent in the sense of believing that you have control and influence over your own experience.

- You would believe that you could influence your state and health by the way you think.

- You would be capable of generating whatever state you want in yourself, relaxation, excitement, peace, confidence.

- You would take care of both your body and your mind and keep them fit.

- You would create the memories and imaginations that you want to have and you would have the ability to do this.

Successful people in sport, in business and in many more fields believe that mind and body are one. They know that by looking after one they are simultaneously looking after the other.

As memory and imagination have the same neurological circuits, they potentially have the same impact.

This belief is at the heart of all NLP teaching. Through NLP we have discovered the details of the way we hold memories and thoughts. We know now that by developing our mastery of the way we represent these thoughts we can change our experience.

Remember your first day at secondary school. How do you remember this? What came to mind first? Was it an image, a memory of someone's voice, a feeling? What followed? Another image? Sounds? What are the qualities of the memory? Is it bright, dark, loud, gentle? Your memory and the way you hold that memory are unique to you. That unique representation is what gives the memory its quality.

Without the representation in your mind it is merely a statement 'first day at secondary school'. What makes it live as a memory is the way you think about it.

KNOWLEDGE, THOUGHT, MEMORY AND IMAGINATION ARE THE RESULT OF SEQUENCES AND COMBINATIONS OF WAYS OF FILTERING AND STORING INFORMATION

How will I ever get to know everyone?

Noise of so many pupils talking at once

First day at Secondary School

Picture of the school

Coolness of the assembly hall

Teacher says 'Welcome to Aigburth Vale grammar School. This is a milestone in your life'

For me this is an exciting memory, also a slightly scary one. What I have illustrated here is the way I represent that memory and I can, if I choose, change any part of it in the way I think about it. I can turn up the brightness. I can imagine the teacher saying different words. I can change the order of the thoughts.

'Con' tricks

Now imagine tomorrow at work. What does your imagination conjure up for you? Successes? Problems? Satisfaction? Frustrations? Does your imagination create for you a representation of the 'tomorrow' that you would like to have? It's all a 'con trick' of the mind, so why not 'con' yourself positively? You can change these representations, so that you have the imagined day that you want to have.

Turn this:

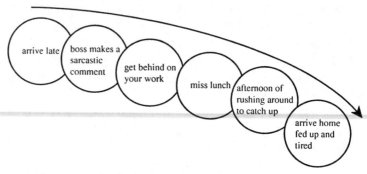

To this:

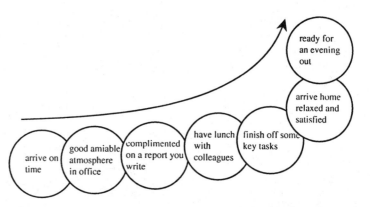

It may not happen exactly like this, but you've increased the chances that it will and you'll feel differently in your anticipation of the day than you would if you thought the first way. Managing your thinking process is at the heart of being able to manage yourself. Many of the subsequent sections will address how to do this.

PRESUPPOSING THE LIFE YOU WANT

Consider the beliefs of excellence. These are the beliefs held by people who achieve excellence in their life.

Imagine trying on a new outfit of clothes. You can have them for as long as you want, so that you can discover how they feel, whether they look the way you want them to look, what reactions you get from people around you and whether they fit. If you don't like them you can return them and wear your original clothes, or you might keep one or two items and wear them with some of your existing clothes. Or you can keep them and make them a part of your wardrobe.

Beliefs are like this. You can presuppose that they are true for you, you can 'try them on'. If they work then it is likely that they will become a belief. If not you can put them to one side. To help you do this use Chapter 3.6 in the Toolkit, Take on a Belief of Excellence.

'Try on' beliefs

BELIEFS THAT UNDERPIN APPRAISAL

It is valuable to explore the beliefs from which you operate not only as an individual but also as an organisation. For example, if part of a company appraisal scheme is to review performance against a manager's ability to discipline (as I experienced in one company), then there is a belief that discipline will be necessary in that organisation. When you see a van or lorry with the inscription 'If you have any problems with the way this vehicle is driven please phone...', the belief is that there are drivers who will drive badly.

However, beliefs that support appraisal schemes that work, and by that I mean ones that result in motivated staff who learn to improve their performance, consist of:

- People have all the resources they need to achieve what they want. Managers who hold this belief are likely to facilitate their staff's development through questioning and coaching rather than telling them what to do.

- People make the best choice available to them at the time that they make it. This does not mean that you have to accept the choice that they made. However, managers who do hold this belief will be more understanding in the way they deal with the jobholder who has made a mistake.

- There is no failure, only feedback. Imagine a company in which all the employees held this belief. It would be an organisation with a climate of total honesty, openness and learning. This is the key to performance improvement.

- The meaning of the communication is its effect. For 'communication' you could substitute 'management', i.e. the meaning of the way you manage your staff is the results they achieve. If a manager's staff are achieving, that is a statement about the ability of the manager. Equally, if the staff are performing badly this is also a measure of the manager's ability to manage. The second part of this belief runs: 'If what you are doing isn't working, do something different.' This is a useful point to bear in mind and act on if your appraisal system isn't achieving what you want it to achieve.

True beliefs

It is valuable to have all the beliefs of excellence. The ones above are ones that seem to have the most relevance to performance management. A company needs to develop its own beliefs. They will only work, however, if they are the true beliefs of the people who work for that organisation. One of the most valuable things a company top team can do is to explore the actual beliefs held by the management team and decide if these are the ones that support their future vision.

BELIEFS AT THE HEART OF CUSTOMER CARE

Many organisations have invested in customer care training. However, sending out a questionnaire and teaching staff to smile as they greet you will not go far with your customers unless customer care is an integral part of everything you do. Does the concept of customer care run through everything you do or is it only surface deep?

Integration

Customer care is an integral part of you and your organisation if you hold beliefs that support your thinking about your customer. A specific set of beliefs that support caring for your customer are:

- The response you get is a measure of the service you provide.

- Whatever your customer says and does to you has a benefit to your business. This is true if you accept there is a potential benefit to you in any situation.

- There is no failure, only feedback. Knowing and acting on feedback will keep you in touch with your customers and will ensure your business meets and even anticipates their needs.

- Each person is unique. By understanding and relating to that uniqueness you will earn your customers' respect.

- Whatever your customers' circumstances, by believing that there is a solution to every problem you will find new and creative solutions with which to progress.

By holding beliefs such as these, you will learn how to deal with your customers appropriately. Chapter 3.7 in the Toolkit contains a customer care checklist which includes thinking about beliefs, and also incorporates references to all other relevant NLP techniques.

BELIEFS THAT SUPPORT NEGOTIATION

Skilled negotiators, those who are able to resolve conflict and bring situations to a solution that has the commitment of all parties involved, believe the following:

- It is desirable and possible for all parties to meet their needs in negotiation.

- The other parties have ideas and views that can benefit everyone.

- I have a positive intention towards the other parties and whatever they say or do has a benefit for me if I choose to open my mind to what that might be.

- We all have a common goal even if we don't yet know what it is.

SUMMARY

Beliefs are emotionally held thoughts about ourselves, others and situations. They are not based on fact but on our perception of events at the time they were formed. In studying figures of excellence we find certain core beliefs which underpin their ability to excel and achieve. These are the beliefs of excellence.

We can step into (presuppose) these beliefs and experience the consequences of holding them to be true. By trying them out and finding the ones that work for us we can, over time, turn them into beliefs for ourselves.

Once upon a time there was a young prince who believed in all things but three. He did not believe in princesses, or in islands or in God. His father, the King, told him that such things did not exist. There were no princesses or islands in his father's domain, and no sign of God. The young prince believed his father.

One day, the prince ran away from his palace to the next country. There, to his astonishment, from every coast he saw islands, and on these islands, strange and troubling creatures whom he dared not name. As he was searching for a boat, a man in full evening dress approached him along the shore.

'Are those real islands?' asked the young prince.

'Of course they are real islands,' said the man in evening dress.

'And those strange and troubling creatures?'

'They are all genuine and authentic princesses.'

'Then God must also exist!' cried the prince.

'I am God,' replied the man in full evening dress, with a bow.

The young prince returned home as quickly as he could.

'So you are back,' said his father, the King.

'I have seen islands, I have seen princesses, I have seen God,' said the prince reproachfully.

The King was unmoved.

'Neither real islands, nor real princesses, nor a real God, exist.'

'I saw them!'

'Tell me how God was dressed.'

'God was in full evening dress.'

'Were the sleeves of his coat rolled back?'

The prince remembered that they had been. The King smiled.

'That is the uniform of a magician. You have been deceived.'

At this the prince returned to the next land, and went to the same shore, where once again he came upon the man in full evening dress.

'My father, the King, has told me who you are,' said the young prince indignantly. 'You deceived me last time, but not again. Now I know that those are not real islands and real princesses, because you are a magician.'

The man on the shore smiled.

'It is you who are deceived, my boy. In your father's kingdom there are many islands and many princesses. But you are under your father's spell, so you cannot see them.'

The prince returned pensively home, when he saw his father he looked him in the eyes.

'Father, is it true that you are not a real King, but only a magician?'

The King smiled and rolled back his sleeves.

'Yes my son, I am only a magician.'

'I must know the real truth, the truth beyond magic.'

'There is no truth beyond magic,' said the King.

The prince was full of sadness. He said, 'I will kill myself.'

The King, by magic caused death to appear. Death stood in the door and beckoned to the real prince. The prince shuddered. He remembered the beautiful but unreal islands and the unreal but beautiful princesses.

'Very well,' he said. 'I can bear it.'

'You see, my son,' said the King, 'you too now begin to be a magician.'

The Magus, © John Fowles, Jonathan Cape, 1977.

Reprinted with permission.

2.2 Create a Compelling Vision — Well Formed Outcomes

Compelling goals

How compelling are your goals? Many organisations invest millions in objective setting and appraisal schemes. Maybe you have experienced this. If so, are the goals that you set as part of this process in your desk drawer or in the forefront of your mind providing a focus for everything that you do? You may be familiar with many different objective-setting schemes. Objectives that need to be SMART: Specific, Measurable, Achievable, Realistic and Time bound; or end results that can be measured in terms of quantity, quality, time, cost and behaviour. And back to the question. Are they compelling, are they the source of motivation and inspiration for you? They should be. Yet the reality is often far from this.

People who achieve what they want in life have compelling goals. The NLP process of modelling high achievers, people, teams and organisations who consistently achieve the goals they set themselves, has pinpointed the difference that makes the difference, the difference between the ritualistic goal setting that ends up in the bottom drawer and the compelling visions that uplift and motivate individuals and organisations alike. NLP has enabled us to decode the qualities of these compelling visions and reproduce them for ourselves.

'All men dream: but not equally. Those who dream by night in the dusty recesses of their minds wake in the day to find that it was vanity: but

the dreamers of the day are dangerous men, for they may act their
dreams with open eyes, to make it possible.'

T E Lawrence

Let's take some examples:

Kevin was constantly searching for success. He'd had eight different jobs
in five years. Each had failed to meet his expectations. Each time he'd
fallen out with his manager and the market conditions for each business
had not been 'quite right'. 'Customers just aren't coming through the
door,' he stated frequently. Lack of success certainly wasn't due to lack of
effort. Kevin tried very hard. He was constantly busy, in fact he rarely
had time to spare for anything else. He regularly talked about it being 'a
tough world out there' and yet each new challenge resulted in the same
familiar disappointment. He talked about not wanting to make the same
mistakes again, particularly in terms of his choice of business and
manager, but somehow he always did.

* * *

Jim worked for a large organisation. He had fulfilled his particular
ambitions by continuing in the family tradition of engineering. Although
he had developed quickly within the organisation he somehow felt that the
job he had wasn't quite what he wanted to do, but he wasn't really sure
what that was. He felt as though he was constantly searching for what his
future might be. Initiative and ambition, particularly in younger
managers, were generally frowned upon although Jim's own manager had
been supportive towards him. His family, however, were pleased with what
they considered to be his success. In their terms he had done well.

THE CONDITIONS

How is it that Kevin consistently repeats the patterns of his
past? What is missing for Jim? What will make the difference?

In contrast:

Jill worked for a large organisation and was clear that although the
organisation was slow and bureaucratic in its style, she wanted to stay
and make a difference. She wanted to be a key player in the
management of change towards a culture that was more open, supportive
and honest than at present. She recognised that her level of influence in
her current role was limited and had mapped out the future roles she
wanted that would increase that influence to introduce the changes she
believed to be important. She knew that if she waited for others to make
this happen she might wait forever. There were also many significantly

older managers in the company.

One thing that struck you about Jill when you met her was that she wanted passionately to achieve this future. Her face lit up and her eyes sparkled as she talked about what was important to her. She spoke positively of what she wanted and was respectful of other people's views and opinions. People enjoyed her company.

What precisely was the difference in the way Jill thought about her outcomes and the way Kevin and Jim thought about theirs? Jill was certainly on track to achieve her outcome.

How is it that some people are satisfied, highly motivated and consistently achieving the sort of success they want? What exactly is the difference? Let's explore this in a way that will enable you both to set compelling outcomes for yourself and to facilitate the outcomes of others.

KNOW WHAT YOU WANT

'Until one is committed, there is hesitancy, the chance to draw back, always ineffectiveness. Concerning all acts of initiative and creation, there is one fact, one elementary truth, the ignorance of which kills countless ideas and splendid plans. That the moment that one definitely commits oneself then providence moves too. All sorts of things to help one that would never otherwise have occurred manifest themselves. A whole stream of events issue from the decision, raising in one's favour all manner of unforeseen incidents and meetings and material assistances that no man could have dreamed would have come his way.'

W H Murray

Consider this statement: 'DON'T THINK ABOUT KANGAROOS!' Can you *not* do that? I doubt it. Your unconscious mind cannot recognise negatives. When you tell yourself not to worry or not to make a mistake, you are actually programming yourself to do just that. However, if you program yourself to think about being calm or getting things right, then you are dramatically increasing the chances that that is what you will be or do.

Program yourself

Top sports people have learned this lesson well. They know that if they start worrying about hitting the ball out of court or off the green then that is probably what will happen. How often have you said to yourself 'I mustn't do that' only to find yourself doing 'that'? Successful sports people know that they are more likely to achieve the performance and therefore the results they want if they imagine what they do want. They have 'modelled' themselves on excellence.

What you think influences how you feel and how you communicate.

Two teams had been given the job of identifying ways in which their business could pull itself out of recession and achieve new business objectives that had been set. The teams had been asked to develop their ideas and to return on a specific date to present their conclusions. They returned with new proposals as agreed.

One team looked dejected. They presented their ideas, how to cut costs, reduce overheads and rationalise the workforce. They felt this was the way forward. An air of gloom hung around them. The rest of the room was silent.

The second team presented their ideas. They looked delighted. This team was made up of people from the manufacturing side of the business. Previously they had looked at ways of improving quality and reducing wastage. This time they had decided to take a different stance. They had thought about the future that they really wanted, the number of plants they would like to build, the amount of research they wanted to do and the people they wanted to employ. They were fired up with their ideas and their passion for the future. They had decided it was time to turn the company around. It should be they who were telling the salesforce how much business they needed to support this programme, instead of them responding to whatever the salesforce would sell as had been the case in the past.

The difference in the enthusiasm and sheer energy of the two teams was dramatic. One had thought about what they had to cut back and lose and the other about what they really wanted. Naturally, if you think about what you don't want you can become disheartened. You will develop the feelings and responses that are triggered by being in an environment of circumstances and people and events that you don't like. It is no surprise that if you think about what you really want, if you imagine what it is like to have what you really want, then you will be committed, you will be motivated and you will be influential because your enthusiasm will be infectious. This is one of the reasons why visionary leaders are compelling.

Visionary leaders

Ask yourself the question: 'What do I really want?'

- today?
- tomorrow?
- this year?
- next year?
- in the next five years?

- in my career?

- in my life?

If you get some shoulds/oughts/musts/try tos creeping in, banish them. They are not a part of this thinking. When you think of what you *should* do, you are often thinking in terms of what other people in your life, past and present, think you should do. This thinking is about what you really want for yourself. You may feel uncomfortable with that, especially if you're not used to asking yourself that question.

Compare how you feel when you think in terms of 'must' as opposed to 'really want'. Think of something you feel you 'must' do. Imagine it. How do you feel? Now think of something you 'really want'. Immerse yourself in it. How does that feel? Usually thinking about anything that you should, must or ought to do carries a tension with it, whereas what you really want can generate feelings of excitement, delight and enthusiasm. Asking yourself what you really want is about being true to yourself.

KNOW WHEN YOU'VE GOT THERE

What will it be like to have what you really want? If you can imagine it then it is virtually yours. The more you step into this imagined future the more you are programming yourself to get there. Think again about one of the outcomes you really want for yourself.

What does it look like?	What do you see? What is around you? Is there anyone else in the picture? Look around, take in the details.
What does it sound like?	What do you hear? What are you saying to yourself? What are others saying? What sounds are there?
What does it feel like?	What can you touch and what sort of feeling is that? What emotions do you feel?

Act as if it is true

Your unconscious mind does not differentiate between what is imagined and what is real. The more vividly you imagine yourself achieving what you want, the more your unconscious mind believes it already has it and will program you to act as if you do. And of course, the more you act as if you have it the more likely you are to get it!

Once you have established your outcome in all your senses in this way, it begins to take on a momentum of its own. This ability to step into your outcome is characteristic of NLP. The difference comes from being able to imagine yourself (associate) into the future that you want. Although planning to get there is important, the steps in the plan will almost begin to present themselves to you automatically because you will begin to recognise opportunities when they occur.

It is likely that you will want your outcome in some situations but not others. For example, if you want a feeling of certainty and self-confidence this could be very appropriate when giving a presentation or when planning your future, but inappropriate in a situation where you had some partly formed ideas and wanted your colleagues to develop their own thinking about these ideas.

PUT IT IN CONTEXT

So ensure you put your outcome in context. Where, when and with whom do you want your outcome?

KEEP IT UNDER YOUR CONTROL

In the case study at the beginning of this chapter, one of the reasons Kevin did not achieve his goals was that they depended on others and on external circumstances. When he didn't achieve what he wanted it was because his manager or the business climate or his customers weren't quite right. He had not asked himself how he could be different whatever the external circumstances. He wanted others to be different. A useful question here is to ask yourself, 'What kind of person do I want to become?'

Where is your attention in relation to your outcomes? On yourself or on others? Do your outcomes depend on someone else being there or responding in a certain way? If so, they are not self-maintained. There is a lovely story in *Waiting for the Mountain to Move* by Charles Handy in which he describes a traveller who, journeying around the world, came to a road and across this road was a mountain blocking the way. The traveller sat down and waited for the mountain to move. If your outcomes are not self-maintained then you too will be waiting for the mountain to move!

Letting go

If your outcome does depend on someone or something else, sometimes this can be the painful part. Can you let go of that need to have someone or something else change? Once you can, then in a strange way you increase the chances that you can have what you really want.

IS IT WORTH WHAT IT TAKES?

What will it take to achieve what you want?

- Risk?

- Feelings of discomfort?

- Giving up something you have now?

- Pain and sadness?

Is having the outcome worth what it takes? You may decide it is not, in which case you can give it up or decide to go for a part or a variation of the outcome. If you decide the outcome is worth what it takes, you are making a decision to commit and to proceed to the next step.

WHAT DOES YOUR PRESENT STATE DO FOR YOU?

In some ways your present state will satisfy a need you have. If it didn't, you wouldn't maintain it. Think carefully about how your present state serves you. It may seem odd but, for example, someone who wants to be fit and healthy may find that being unhealthy gets them sympathy and attention. Equally, someone who is non-assertive but who wants to be assertive may find that being non-assertive is a way of avoiding risk and responsibility. It is important to consider these needs and either how you will challenge them or meet them in different ways in the future in a way that leaves you free to achieve your outcome.

UNDERSTAND YOUR HIGHER PURPOSE

How do you turn an outcome that isn't self-maintained into one that is? One way is to find out what you want it for. What's important to you about achieving this outcome?

For example, Kevin wanted more customers to come to *his* door. He wanted the recession to ease. Neither of these are self-maintained. They both come into the category of 'waiting for the mountain to move'.

By asking the question 'What's important about achieving these outcomes?', Kevin identified that he wanted to generate more business. Now the outcome begins to become self-maintained. At this higher level it opens up the possibilities of ways in which he can achieve this.

Moving up levels in this way is referred to as 'chunking up'. You may find it useful to 'chunk up' a number of times to find the most meaningful outcome for you.

For Kevin 'chunking up' resulted in the following:

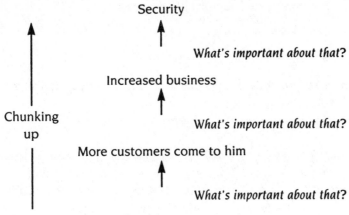

Security

What's important about that?

Increased business

What's important about that?

Chunking
up

More customers come to him

What's important about that?

Recession to ease

At the higher levels the outcomes become more centred on Kevin and therefore more within his influence. Checking out these higher level outcomes also ensures that you put your outcome into context and that it does indeed meet a higher level purpose for you. Each success becomes a stepping stone to a higher level outcome. Success builds on success. You avoid the post-success emptiness that some people feel when they achieve outcomes that don't lead on to something else.

Peter had achieved great success in developing a professional presentation style on a training course. When the group commented on how impressed his team back at work would be with his new skills, he responded, 'You must be joking. I'd stand out like a sore thumb if I used this style back at work.'

ENSURE YOUR OUTCOMES FIT WITH WHO YOU ARE AND WHO YOU WANT TO BE

Having these skills did not fit with the person that Peter considered himself to be back at work. The likelihood that he would ever use them was minimal.

Check out your outcomes with the kind of person you are or want to be. If they don't fit forget them, find ones that do. Only by doing this will you ensure that every part of you is 'rooting' for your success.

'Whatever you can do or dream you can do, begin it. Boldness has genius and power and magic in it. Begin it now!'

Goethe

TAKE ACTION

What action steps will you take? What steps are realistic for you? I see so many action plans on company appraisal forms that have grand statements such as:

- Improve managerial effectiveness.

- Develop better communication.

- Build an effective team.

This sort of statement is 'pie in the sky'. It means nothing and it comes to nothing.

Small steps are the way forward.

Small steps to success

When I set myself an outcome of buying a home in Wiltshire it seemed like a major decision. It was frightening when I thought of all that it entailed for me at that time. My action steps were very small. Each one felt safe at the time I took it. My plan was:

1. *Find out what sort of magazines/brochures would have details of the kind of house I wanted. (I didn't even buy the magazines at this stage.)*
2. *Register with the sort of estate agents who had details of this type of property. At this stage I made it clear I didn't want to view any properties.*
3. *Drive through the areas where I thought I might want to live.*
4. *Visit one or two chosen properties but on the clear understanding that I was not ready to buy.*

and so on...

It was a year from the time I started this process to the time I found a house I wanted to buy. Each step was a realistic one for me at that time. The result was that I found a cottage with which I and my family fell in love.

It helps to set a time frame for each of your action steps. Give yourself a date by which you will have achieved each one. It may not always be necessary to know them all in advance, but set out the first one or two. This way you will have started your journey towards your outcome.

To apply all the preceding principles of well formed outcomes you can refer to Chapter 3.9 of the Toolkit, Prioritise Your Goals as Well Formed Outcomes. To find out how you stop yourself from achieving what you want and how to overcome these stoppers, read Chapter 3.10.

ORGANISATIONAL OUTCOMES

The characteristics of well formed outcomes work in just the same way for organisations as for individuals.

Reactive culture

Problem centred organisations are ones that are moving away from what they don't want. These organisations are more likely to 'react' to the competition and in so doing become dependent on what the 'competition' does next. They are driven by market trends and are directly affected by the economic climate. They step into a 'fire-fighting', crisis based way of working. Their goals are set in reaction to others. They have difficulty planning and sticking to any plans they do manage to set. Their actions are determined by what other companies do next. Organisations functioning solely in this way cannot maintain success for long. The climate inside a company of this style is typically one of tension and worry.

Proactive culture

Outcome oriented organisations, on the other hand, have a clear vision of where they are heading. This vision is an expression of what the employees in this company really want. Because of this there is a high level of motivation and commitment to the future. Staff enjoy their work. The vision is an inspiration both to those who work within the company and to those with whom they come into contact, their customers, their suppliers. This style of company sets market trends. It influences its customers to move forward with them to their vision of the future. Outcome oriented companies are innovative and influential. They do take account of market trends, the economic climate and competitors, but they do this in the context of having a clear compelling outcome and business plans.

IMAGE AND OUTCOMES

A great deal of attention has been paid to 'image' in recent years, personal, professional and corporate image. The business world has become much more image conscious. Image is the impression you create on everyone around you. Each person develops their own unique impression of you depending on what is important to them in the way they experience the world. Someone who communicates their image congruently is effectively signalling their outcomes to the world at large. Not surprisingly, the world signals back by providing opportunities in line with these outcomes. Coincidence is a measure of a congruent expression of outcomes and values. For example, when you meet someone unexpectedly who meets your core values and seems to fit with your thinking about your direction, it is as a result of the way you have unconsciously signalled your outcomes and your values to the world at large.

Some of the thinking about image has been done at a superficial level by considering only style of clothes and type of non-verbal behaviour. If you want to communicate an image that is a true expression of what you want and what is important to you, then NLP is the difference that makes the difference. It is the more subtle elements of behaviour that communicate your true image.

Image comes from within

Your thoughts and your feelings are the source of your image. What you think and what you feel will influence your movement, your facial expression, your voice, everything that you say and do. These thoughts and feelings leak out of every pore in your body, you cannot conceal them. People around you do not need to *learn* to be 'body language experts' to read these signals, they already are. Even if your conscious mind doesn't pick up the signals your unconscious mind will. For example:

Image signals

- Where exactly do you look when you move your eyes?

- What tiny muscle changes take place in your face and your body as you talk and as you move?

- How does the colour in the exposed parts of your face and body change as you communicate?

- Precisely what patterns exist in the way you use language?

- How does your breathing change in different situations?

- What muscle movements occur that are beyond your conscious awareness?

It is these things that convey your core image and the only way you can change them, if you choose to, is by changing that core image. These tiny messages are the way your deeply felt emotions and thoughts are leaked out to the world at large.

And the world at large picks them up and responds to them.

Your experience is an expression of who you are.

The first question you need to ask yourself is what image you want for yourself. The more you know what you really want and the more you imagine yourself (associate into) achieving this outcome, the more it will show itself in how you speak and how you act. This is when you will begin to detect opportunities. This is not coincidence, although it might seem so at the time. This is the result of you sending non-verbal signals to the world at large and the world responding.

Some people would say that an image is a façade. It can be if you attempt to adopt a façade that isn't an expression of who you really are and especially who you really want to be. The image we are describing here is an expression of your outcomes for yourself. More important than that, your ability to manifest your outcomes in your behaviour will affect the success you have in achieving those outcomes.

The essence of who you are

Calvin Klein is in the 'image business'. His clothes, his perfumes are all designed to help you create an 'image'. He was the subject of a marketing programme I saw on television some time ago. In this programme he was explaining how the style of the clothes he designed had evolved. He described his range of perfumes, in particular 'Eternity' and the most recent one at that time, 'Escape'.

As he talked about the perfumes he exuded his passion for the significance of the scent, the name and the way it was packaged. The perfumes were expressions of himself. He didn't have to work at selling his products. He lived it.

This is what image is all about. Find out how you can express your true image by turning to Chapter 3.11 of the Toolkit.

LEADING THE WAY WITH CUSTOMER CARE

One of the biggest shifts in business has been the move towards customer care and customer satisfaction. NLP, and in particular outcome thinking, can have a dramatic impact on the effect you have on your customers. It is the precision and discipline of outcome thinking that can make the difference between customer satisfaction (or dissatisfaction) and customer delight.

We're in a world of high speed change and innovation. It is the people and companies who can initiate and introduce change who stay ahead. They are the leaders, the influencers. If you lack vision then you can only react to the changes that

Initiating change

others impose. Having a well formed outcome allows you to create your own future.

If you have a vision for the future that is compelling for you then it will become compelling for others for whom it is relevant. Well formed outcomes are a way of creating a compelling vision. If you can do this for yourself, you can do this for your role in your company and for the business itself.

Customer delight

Step into the future and imagine how you would really like it to be. Imagine your customers in this future. What does 'customer delight' look like, sound like, feel like from your perspective? By developing your skill to step into a future that you really want, you will be unleashing your creativity and productivity. It is these qualities that lead and influence others. Customer delight is a proactive not a reactive process.

WHAT YOU MEASURE IS WHAT YOU GET

So how do you measure customer satisfaction?

Reduction or absence of complaints	Amount of praise received for a job well done
Number of problems solved	Number of thank-yous for the service you give
Reduction in time taken to deal with customer calls	Voluntary feedback on the benefits that have resulted
Extent to which you can keep customers off your back	from using your service or product
Amount of resource allocated to your customer	Amount of repeat business
	Evidence of improvement on the customers' work processes
	Amount of smiling and fun

Brickbats or bouquets

The column on the left contains some very traditional ways of measuring customer satisfaction. They are typically 'problem based'. If your customer satisfaction measures are expressed in terms of what you don't want that is where you will put your attention and that is exactly what you will get. If you measure complaints, this presupposes that is what you expect and sure enough, that is what you will get!

I returned from a very enjoyable cycling holiday to find a 'customer care' questionnaire waiting for me. In it I was asked to say not 'What was my opinion of the overnight accommodation?' but 'What problems did I experience with the accommodation?' What did I do? I immediately began to search in my memory for problems that might have existed.

Through their questionnaire they were directing me to remember and even 'dig for' the unsatisfactory elements of my holiday.

So, using the principles of outcome thinking, think of what you do really want in your relationships with your customers and how you will know, in sensory specific terms, when you have achieved it.

What you measure is what you get.

SUMMARY

Outcome thinking is a very powerful approach to achieving what you want. The elements of outcome thinking are drawn from people in all walks of life who consistently achieve what they want in a way that is compatible both with those around them and with their environment. By following the steps to setting a well formed outcome you are modelling the way these successful people think about outcomes. By imagining yourself achieving what you want in all senses you are programming yourself to get what you want. Your mind cannot distinguish between what is imagined and what is real, so you are managing your imagination to work for you in a way that makes your dreams become your reality.

This way of thinking works in all situations and at all levels, from setting an outcome for a five-minute discussion to establishing a vision for a company. The success comes from ensuring that your thinking about your outcomes meets all the conditions for a well formed outcome. Each element is crucial to the eventual likelihood of success.

THOUGHT PROVOKERS
1 Are the following towards or away from? 　　a.　I really want a job that involves me working with other people. 　　b.　The company I work for currently is very bureaucratic. I want somewhere else to work. 　　c.　I have a clear vision of myself working abroad.
2 You ask another department to agree a level of service with you. When you have explained what you need they say they will try to meet your requirements. How confident would you be that they would deliver?

3   What was the basis of your decision to take your existing job? Were you moving towards your ideal or away from something you didn't like? And your previous job?

4   Imagine yourself doing the type of work that you would really like to do. What can you see/hear/feel?

5   Think of examples of action plans you have set yourself in the past. What is characteristic of the action plans that you have carried out compared with the ones you haven't?

6   How do you decide how to spend your holidays? How well does the reality match up to your expectations?

7   How often do you finish up with the things you don't want compared with the things you do?

8   Think about what you would really like to achieve by the end of this week. Pay attention to what is in your mind. Is it what you do want or are you imagining the problems of the things you don't want?

Once upon a time there was a man and wife. This couple had achieved many of their ambitions in life yet there was one main goal outstanding. They wanted to swim to Japan.

They thought about this and one day they set off. They were not used to swimming so they found it difficult. They were aware of how heavy their limbs felt. They ached with the constant effort, especially when the strong current was against them. Gradually, however, their bodies got used to swimming and they developed a style that became effortless and rhythmical.

They began to notice the water around them, how it changed colour as the days went by. In the early morning it would be clear and blue and in certain lights it sparkled emerald green. As the sun set it developed the rich warm colours of the evening sky. And they became aware of the creatures in the water, the small silver fish that swam with them in the day, the dark shadows that skimmed by them in the deep. They became aware of how the sound of the waves changed as it lapped their ears and they felt the subtle changes of the weather as breezes turned into winds and died down again. They learned how to find food in the water, how to nourish themselves and how to use their bodies effortlessly. They developed a refined sense of smell so that they could detect changes in the environment by the scent carried to them on the breeze.

They swam for days and weeks with no sight of land. One day they saw the dark profile of land on the horizon. They swam on and they recognised the shoreline of Japan. As they approached they became quiet and eventually they looked at each other and they knew. At that moment they turned back to the sea and swam on.

2.3 Develop a Climate of Trust — Rapport

Decisions

Rapport is the ability to relate to others in a way that creates a climate of trust and understanding. Rapport is the ability to see each other's point of view (not necessarily to agree with it), to be on the same wavelength and to appreciate each other's feelings. It is a vital element in any form of communication — unless, of course, you don't want to make progress! Most business decisions are made on the basis of rapport rather than technical merit; not only instant rapport but also rapport that has been built up in a relationship over time. You are more likely to buy from, agree with, support someone you can relate to than someone you can't.

The skills involved in building and maintaining rapport were some of the earliest to be discovered with NLP. The people who were chosen as models of excellence, particularly in situations of influence or change, demonstrated that one of the most important factors that needed to exist for change to take place was rapport.

This is true in most situations today. Many management systems flounder not because of the system itself but because the company attempts to install the system without there being good rapport between the managers and their staff. Rapport is a prerequisite to good communication, influence and change. NLP practitioners determine the fine distinctions in behaviour that lead to the existence of rapport.

There have been many studies of rapport that exist only at the level of body language. However, in modelling people who achieve deep levels of rapport we now know that the skill to build and maintain rapport goes well beyond the level of body language. The levels of awareness achieved through NLP provide a means to build and maintain deep levels of rapport that can enhance the quality of your relationships.

Quality in relationships

Alan had dreaded his meeting with a manager who was renowned as an ogre. As part of his introductory NLP training Alan planned how he might handle this manager. He developed his rapport building skills. When the meeting actually happened Alan got on with this manager like a 'house on fire'!

HOW TO BUILD AND MAINTAIN RAPPORT

Think of someone with whom you feel you do have good rapport. What is true about your contact with them that isn't true for others? If you are in the company of other people, look around you. Who has rapport with their colleagues? Who does not?

Pay attention to how they are physically. People in rapport typically adopt the same posture, move and gesture in similar ways, laugh together, adopt the same style and rhythm in movement and speech. They 'match' each other. This happens naturally when two or more people are in rapport. They probably aren't consciously aware of it happening. The result of this is that their thinking and feelings will be similar. Have you ever had that uncanny experience of having someone say exactly what you were thinking, or find that you know exactly what someone else is feeling? It's not surprising that if you adopt the same physical posture as someone else that you will experience similar feelings.

People like people who are like themselves

One of the core beliefs consistently held by early models of excellence is that:

Mind and body are part of the same system. What occurs in one part will affect all the other parts.

By modelling people who had deep levels of rapport it was discovered that this occurs when the people in the interaction adopted the same or similar style of:

- posture;

- movement and gestures;

- breathing levels;

- voice tone and quality;

- language content — visual/auditory/feelings, and key words;

- beliefs;

- values.

Adopting the same style

The ability to take on the same style as someone else is known as **matching**.

Bill was a systems analyst and headed up a team of analysts. He dealt with many other departments in the company and frequently accompanied members of the sales team in meetings with clients. Technically he was highly skilled but he didn't feel at ease in the company of others. He had attended many training courses on the techniques of running effective meetings, making presentations, communicating confidently, but he still didn't enjoy most situations where he had to talk to other people, especially those that involved meeting people for the first time. He could get on well with people he had known for some time but initial meetings he found stressful.

The result of this was that the clients tended to direct their conversations away from Bill. Occasionally he met with someone with whom he seemed to 'click' straight away, but this wasn't often. The emphasis in his role was changing. He increasingly accompanied members of the sales team on customer visits. As such he needed to make a good first impression.

Rapport is essential for any meaningful communication to take place. You need rapport to be able to conduct a productive conversation, to hold an informative interview, to run an effective meeting. Without rapport very little communication of value will occur.

'Just because you are making a noise in my direction don't think you are communicating.'

David Gordon

Building rapport

So what happens when rapport doesn't naturally occur? This is when the skill of rapport building is crucial. People skilled at building rapport are able quickly to put others at ease in their company. Let's explore the characteristics of people who are able to build exquisite rapport.

Excellent communicators build rapport by:

- paying conscious attention to matching those elements that are part of natural rapport;

- matching any and as many as possible of the following:

Posture	position of the body/position of the legs and feet/weight distribution position of the arms/hands/fingers how the shoulders are held inclination of the head
Expression	direction of the look movement of the gaze
Breathing	rate of breathing position of the breathing, in the chest/abdomen or low stomach
Movement	everyone has what can be called a signature rhythm, match the pace of this, fast/steady/slow/still
Voice	pace/volume/pitch/tone/type of words intonation
Language patterns	visual/auditory/feelings

A deep level of rapport exists when more of the internal elements and emotions are matched, for example beliefs and values.

This can be a long list to attempt to work on at one time. Some of these may come naturally to you. Choose one of the less natural ones for you and practise that until you can do it automatically. Choose occasions to practise matching when you are an observer and do not have to engage in conversation.

Be prepared, however. One of my friends who sat silently matching the behaviour of a manager who was engaged in conversation with the friend's colleague was taken by surprise when the manager turned to my friend and said, 'I'd really like to know what you think'! It's amazing what results you get when you have rapport.

Silent rapport

RAPPORT AS A FORM OF INFLUENCE

Rapport is a form of influence. When you are communicating with someone else you are part of a system. The quality of the rapport that you have will influence the communication.

This usually doesn't need much conscious attention. When you have rapport you know it, you feel at ease in the other person's company, conversation flows and equally silence is comfortable. What occurs is like a dance: as one moves the other follows. It is impossible to tell who is leading and who is following as you naturally seek to match the other. Conversation is easy as you understand the meaning and intention of what the other person says. You appreciate each other's feelings. It does not mean that you necessarily agree with everything the other person is saying but you understand what they say.

Pacing

Pacing is another element in rapport building. It is about respecting the state, style or feeling of others. For example, if someone is feeling concerned, to pace them is to show understanding for that concern. If someone is having fun, to pace that would be to enter into that fun with them.

When you can match and pace, you can then lead. This is what influence is all about.

Examples of how and when you might want to use rapport to lead and influence:

- In a discussion or interview with someone who is nervous or hesitant, to help them to relax and open up.

- When you want to introduce new ways of working to an individual or department that has become fixed in their thinking.

- When someone is angry, to help them to calm down.

- When someone is worried and tense, to help them relax.

- When you want to teach a new concept, by relating to what people know already.

Match/pace/lead

Match, pace and lead mirrors the martial arts philosophy of going with the movement and using the energy of your partner to take them where you want them to be.

These are some examples of matching, pacing and leading in conversation.

'I can picture the new system that we want to develop.'
'So when you see this system and imagine what it looks like, what are you saying to yourself?'

'I feel uncertain about the customer presentation this afternoon.'

'I can understand that you feel uncertain. How would you like to feel?'

My colleagues told me that they really valued the ideas I put forward at the meeting.'

'When you remember what your colleagues said about the value of your ideas, what do you experience?'

Conversational rapport

Rapport is the crucial factor that makes the difference between the success and failure of most business systems.

It is crucial to **ensure that new systems match the style and culture of the company**. The concept of match, pace, lead works at every level, not only between individuals but when introducing any new element to a system. It is important that any system you introduce fits with what you already have.

Systems that fit

For example, I've sometimes seen small, informal organisations attempt to 'bolt on' the more formal appraisal systems that belong to a much larger, more bureaucratic organisation. One of the simplest and most effective appraisal systems asked only four questions. What are your goals? How well did you do? What skills would help you develop further? What actions shall we commit to? This was successful because the style matched the informality and openness of the company in which it was introduced.

Similarly, it is important to **ensure that rapport exists between the managers and the jobholders**. To continue with appraisal, for a jobholder to accept feedback from his or her manager and vice versa there needs to be rapport. With rapport the appraisal will find its own style and form. Appraisal is about learning and development; it is a vehicle that provides the stimulus for continuous improvement.

MATCHING AND PACING VALUES IN NEGOTIATION

I believe that the need to build and maintain rapport is the most important skill in negotiation. The only outcome at the beginning of a negotiation is to build rapport. From then on it is important to keep a mental check throughout on the level of rapport that exists. Without rapport you have no negotiation. If at any time you lose rapport, rebuild it, and only when you have restored it should you continue. When you have rapport the steps to negotiation become merely reminders as your conversation flows. You take account of each other's point of view. You are open to finding joint solutions.

The negotiations for the Sinai desert were a classic example of how a solution was eventually found by exploring the values of the parties involved. In the peace talks at Camp David, President Sadat and Mr Begin both wanted the Sinai Desert. They were eventually encouraged to explore with each other what was important to them. For Egypt's President Sadat it was sovereignty; this land had always been theirs and was a symbol of their sovereignty. For Mr Begin it was a matter of Israel's security; any occupation of the desert was a threat to their border. This exploration of their values sowed the seeds for the eventual agreement. The Sinai Desert remained under Egyptian sovereignty but it was agreed that it would be unoccupied, which satisfied Mr Begin's need for security. The two sets of values were compatible: they were able to reach a win/win situation.

The negotiations established the core principles on which each side involved made their decisions. By drawing these out and finding a solution that related to these they gained a momentous agreement.

Building on values

Genuine commitment to a solution will only exist if it is built on the values of each of the parties involved. Values are the principles by which you live your life and are core to who you are as a person. Common values bond people together. A partnership, a relationship, a team and a company can unite only if they share common values.

It is not enough to just think about the values of the other party. Respecting and pacing values is a way of building a deep level of rapport. Without this, any other attempts to match and pace are superficial and temporary. Identifying and pacing values is therefore crucial to skilled negotiation. There are different ways to do this. For example, if someone holds the value of security, they will look for a solution to the negotiation that satisfies this value, but they will also want the negotiation to be conducted in a way that respects their need for security. They may, for example, want the points to be presented in a non-threatening way. If someone's value is fun it is possible that they will want their representation of fun to be present both in the way the ideas are put to them and in the solution.

Values are decision factors that affect the everyday situations in which you find yourself. You will, for example, have values on which you make decisions about:

Decision factors

- how to spend your holiday;

- who to believe;

- what job to do;

- who to buy from;

- how to decide whether you have had a good meeting or not.

Your partner in a negotiation will be evaluating you, the venue of the negotiation and the ideas you discuss, among many other things, against their own values. If they judge a person by their ability to listen they will be judging you in just this way. More important than this, they will have a unique way of knowing that each of their values has been met, a set of rules and standards referred to as evidence of fulfilment. Communicators who are considered to be excellent in their ability to achieve understanding and influence are people who can match, pace and lead the other person's values. They identify what conditions have to be true for those values to be satisfied. They operate from the belief that:

Meeting the conditions

Each person is unique

The evidence of fulfilment for each of the following values *could* be (they will be different and unique for everyone):

Value	Evidence of Fulfilment
Openness	A willingness to express feelings. Someone who is prepared to state their views before others state theirs.
Security	Solutions to problems are ones that have been tried and tested and shown to work in other situations. The ability to express ideas without having them ignored or dismissed.

Creativity   Agreements and ideas are ones that haven't been applied before. People who can think laterally and who can provide a new way of thinking about existing situations.

To find out someone's values, watch and listen. What excites them, what changes their state to one of interest and curiosity? To what do they pay attention? If they are constantly looking at their watch and want to get on with discussions straight away, then you may find that attention to time and to the way that time is used is important to them. The more you develop your sensory acuity, your awareness to notice even the smallest of changes in the person with whom you are dealing, the more you will begin to be able to determine when their state changes. Eventually you will be able to 'calibrate' these different patterns of behaviour to the different states so that you know what outward signs symbolise the different states for your partner.

Calibration   One of the surest ways of knowing that you have touched on someone's values will be a skin colour change. If you make a proposal that meets the values and the evidence of fulfilment for the other person, they are very likely to blush. By matching and pacing your partner's values and their evidence of fulfilment you are building a deep level of rapport.

Understanding your own values is a way of beginning to understand those of others. By using Chapter 3.12 of the Toolkit you can establish your core values.

WHOLE BODY LISTENING

Listening with care and curiosity is a rare skill in business. The people who have this ability are usually those who have respect and influence. Rapport is a major component of listening. When you listen with rapport you are listening with your whole body. Not only will you hear what the other person is saying, you will gain insights as to what they are thinking and feeling. You will be influencing the interaction through your non-verbal behaviour alone. As Tom Peters says in his book A *Passion for Excellence*, 'Listening is the highest form of courtesy.' Whole body listening can be the trigger that influences someone to gain insight, to find their own solutions and to generate commitment to those solutions.

External focus   Whole body listening means being able to give all of your attention to someone else. It is the ability to keep your attention external to yourself rather than thinking through your own thoughts. Some textbooks on listening advise you to make 'eye contact'. You can probably remember those situations when, although someone was looking at you, you knew that their mind and spirit were somewhere else entirely! Eye contact alone is no proof of listening. NLP provides the techniques to enable you to listen with your whole body.

Contrast the difference between someone whose attention is internal, i.e. on themselves, and someone who is listening with the whole body.

People whose attention is internal
They think of their own thoughts, make evaluations and judgements. They worry and concentrate on what just happened, what was just said or even what might happen next.

People who are listening with their whole body
They are in a state of curiosity. Their attention is entirely on the other person.

Their intention is towards themselves.

Their intention is towards the other person.

Their gaze may be de-focused or moving around.

Their gaze is on the other person.

The posture could be anything.

They match the other person's posture.

Their language is likely to be 'I', 'me' centred.

Their language is 'you' centred and they use the key words and language patterns that match the person with whom they are speaking.

'I want to talk to you about doing some design work for us. We've worked with one company for a long time now, but they seem to be getting behind the times with their ideas. We've got less time to spend on this than we had in the past, so we want a company who is going to take the initiative to find out what they need to know to give us what we want. We don't have a lot of time and I'd appreciate you telling me whether you genuinely can work in this way with us or not.'

Detecting the clues

Everything that someone says and does will give you some information about their values. They will tell you some explicitly and some may be unknown to them, but they will be there. You only have to look and listen.

So let's say that the values of the speaker in the passage above are:

- effective use of time;

- openness and honesty;

- up to date ideas;

- initiative.

The depth of the rapport you build will depend on your ability to match these values in what you say and what you do. If you start to ramble in the way you respond and if you wait to be asked the next question, you probably won't be very successful.

If, on the other hand, you answer concisely and openly, telling the other person frankly what you can and cannot do, and if you take the lead in asking questions then you will probably make good progress. This will only ring true, however, if they are values that you also hold.

I was talking to a manager of a computer installation at one of our open evenings. He was explaining the problems they had been having with the computer system supplied to them. He also explained that when he raised these problems with the software suppliers they poured people onto the site. I also happen to know the software suppliers and I know that when they did that they believed that they were satisfying that customer's needs. They didn't have a surplus of staff so it was a big decision to put so much resource into one place. How sad then that it wasn't what the customer wanted! They had made a judgement about what to do based on their own values and evidence of fulfilment for customer satisfaction, not those of the client.

What was important to the customer was personal one-to-one reassurance, not only that the current bugs in the system would be fixed but explanations of what the supplier was doing to prevent any similar bugs appearing in the system in the future!

Everyone has their own unique way of satisfying their needs, their evidence of fulfilment. It is crucial to know your customers' evidence of fulfilment and to find ways of meeting them, if you want to succeed in business.

By matching and pacing your customers' values you will draw out their core values, the ones on which they will make their ultimate decision. Here is an example of a conversation that draws out core values and their evidence of fulfilment. It is an example of how it is possible to build rapport through conversation. It will have an even greater effect if you are also matching and pacing all the other elements — non-verbal behaviour, language patterns, beliefs...

Drawing out values

'I'm not really happy with that idea — it would take too much time.'

'OK, I can see that time is important. We can scale it down so that it takes less time. How do you feel about that?' (*pacing their concern for time and leading*)

'Well, I'm not sure because I have made other commitments to my team.'

'I hadn't realised that. Your commitment to your team is a high priority. Maybe we could schedule it in once these commitments have been met.' (*pacing their point about commitment and leading*)

'To be honest I don't feel comfortable that I have all the skills I need to make this work.' (*said congruently*)

An indication that the speaker has reached a core value in thinking is often a change in their state. For example, before talking about a core value, the speaker will often significantly change their physiology. Sometimes this change in state is accompanied by a deep sigh and a change in skin colour.

Sometimes when faced with a concern like this some negotiators dismiss it by saying things such as:

'Oh, I'm sure you've got the skills, don't worry, you'll make it work.'

'You can learn them in no time at all, I've got just the course for you.'

These sorts of statement break rapport by sweeping aside the concerns or by imposing a solution that they believe will work, as opposed to acknowledging the concern and finding out what solution will really meet the other person's needs.

Acknowledge core values

'I respect your honesty and recognition of the need to develop new skills. What would have to be true for you to feel comfortable that you could learn them?'

This is an example of pacing the person's concern about their lack of skill and finding out what would satisfy that need (pacing their core values and questioning to establish their evidence of fulfilment).

Ask your customers the most important question of all — 'What would have to be true for you to want me to be your main supplier for the future?' — and sit back and listen. You will learn some of the most valuable information for meeting your customers' needs that you will ever need to know.

SUMMARY

Rapport is one of the most important elements in effective communication. With rapport others will feel at ease in your company — they will choose to be with you because it is a comfortable experience. By building rapport you build trust and understanding. NLP uncovered the way that skilled communicators and influencers build and maintain rapport.

Building quality

Rapport may exist naturally for you in some situations and with some people. When it doesn't it requires skill to generate it. By taking on the components of rapport building you will be able to reproduce the quality of the relationships that are created by people who are excellent at relating to others and putting them at their ease. Many business decisions are made on the basis of rapport rather than technical merit.

THOUGHT PROVOKERS

1   The next time you are in the company of others pay attention to the elements we have covered in this chapter.

Notice their posture and their movements. Listen to their voice and the words they use.

Identify which people seem to be most in rapport with each other. What similarities are there in these elements?

2   Seek out the company of two people that you know who have excellent rapport with each other. What do you see and hear them doing and saying that are similar?

---

3   Choose one element per day, e.g. head movement, voice tone, body position, etc. Pay attention to that element for each person you meet.

4   Ask a friend to engage in conversation with you. Notice each time your attention changes from external to internal.

Many years ago in the hills of Patagonia there was a tiny village. Its inhabitants were starving. Because they lived in fear of the dragon that they had seen in their fields, they would not go to harvest their crops.

One day a traveller came to the village and when he asked for food they explained that they could not give him any because the dragon kept them from their fields. He was brave and offered to slay the dragon. When he arrived he saw that there was no dragon, only a large watermelon. So he returned to the village and said, 'You have nothing to fear; there is no dragon, only a large watermelon.' The villagers were angry and hacked the traveller to pieces.

Some weeks later another traveller came to the village. Again when he asked for food he was told about the dragon. He too was brave and offered to kill the dragon. The villagers were overjoyed. When he arrived at the fields he also saw the giant watermelon and returned to the village to tell the villagers that they were mistaken about the dragon. They need have no fear of a giant watermelon. They hacked him to pieces.

More time passed and the villagers were becoming desperate. One day a third traveller appeared. He could see how desperate they were and asked what the problem was. They told him and he promised he would slay the dragon so that they could go to the fields to harvest their crops. When he got to the field he too saw the giant watermelon. He drew his sword, leaped into the field and hacked the watermelon to pieces. He returned to the villagers and told them he had killed their dragon — they were delighted. The traveller stayed in the village for many months, long enough to teach the villagers the difference between dragons and watermelons.

2.4 Put Yourself in my Shoes — Perceptual Positions

Some of the original NLP techniques are detailed in their attention to thinking and language patterns. More recently John Grinder and Judith Delozier have developed some new ways of using NLP that are effectively short cuts to achieving excellence. Perceptual positions are a way of appreciating situations from different standpoints. They also form a valuable sequel to Chapter 2.2 on outcome thinking.

Balanced approach

Perceptual positions provide a balanced approach to thinking, not only about outcomes but about any other situation. In situations where you feel there is little or no understanding or progress, perceptual positions can provide a way of developing understanding and creating new choices. This is a very powerful technique for finding congruent solutions that are likely to transform your experience of the whole situation.

There are many different ways of thinking about situations. To begin with it is useful to consider the three primary positions.

1st Position is seeing, hearing and feeling the situation through your own eyes, ears and emotions. You think in terms of what is important to you, what you want to achieve. Your language contains expressions such as 'I feel', 'I want', 'I hear', 'I see'. The 'I' refers to you personally. Essentially you are experiencing the situation as you in your own shoes.

2nd Position   is like stepping into the shoes of the other person and experiencing the situation as if you are them. When you are really in the other person's shoes and not just intellectualising about them, then what you (the other person) are doing and saying makes sense. No matter how bizarre someone's behaviour may seem, in their shoes it is normal. It is the best choice they have. When you are really in 2nd position you use 'I' meaning the other person because for this moment you are them.

3rd Position   is the ability to stand back from a situation and experience it as if you are a detached observer. In your mind, you are able to see and hear yourself and the other person as if you are a third person. It is rather like being a fly on the wall. You are unlikely to have emotions in this position.

To experience what it is like to be in each of these perceptual positions, work through Chapter 3.13 of the Toolkit.

Skilful negotiators instinctively use all three positions as a way of taking a balanced approach to a situation.

IMBALANCED POSITIONS

An imbalanced use of any of the positions has implications for your ability to make progress.

James often had to attend meetings as part of his work. He usually prepared for these meetings by carefully thinking through his proposals. He often had ideas for ways that the department could handle new projects. He couldn't normally see why he wouldn't get the 'go ahead' from his manager. James felt that his manager's style was to stall and throw out objections. James usually felt extremely frustrated by the

Aggression

response he received. As far as he was concerned, his manager was being stubborn. Sometimes his frustration reached such a level that he wondered if it was worth staying with the department.

Excessive use of 1st position can lead to a lack of understanding and subsequent dismissal of other people's feelings and ideas. You might push for the achievement of your outcomes but at the expense of others. So although you may achieve what you want, your achievement is likely to be short lived and may backfire in some way. You may feel overcome by your emotions.

Non-assertion

Diane was considered by her staff to be caring and compassionate. She became concerned if any of her staff experienced problems and would endeavour to help them solve their problems through discussion. However, whenever she did this she found herself experiencing the feelings of whoever it was she was talking to. Not only did she experience these feelings during the discussion, but she found that they stayed with her, often for the rest of the day and sometimes longer.

Excessive use of 2nd position can lead to a loss of self-esteem if you identify with other people's needs and feelings at the expense of your own. Essentially you would be giving others priority over yourself. It is possible that by overly identifying with the other person you stop yourself achieving and even thinking about what you really want. You may find yourself taking on other people's feelings and being unable to shake them off.

Detachment

David was a member of a project team engaged on a high profile task for the company. The project team were working to a tight schedule and sometimes tempers flared and the discussions would become heated. David however, seemed untouched by this emotion. Physically and emotionally he seemed to distance himself. This often irritated the other team members who felt that he didn't care about the success of the project.

Excessive use of 3rd position can give an image of being detached and unemotional. You would be likely to be objective and analytical without the capacity to experience the emotion of the situation. You could liken this position to the style of Mr Spock in *Startrek*.

The ability to use all three positions in a balanced way leads to cooperative, assertive behaviour and increases choice and understanding. Chapter 3.14 of the Toolkit explains how you can use perceptual positions to become more assertive.

WHEN SHOULD YOU USE EACH POSITION?

1st Position   When you want to stand up for yourself, see things from your perspective, hear things for yourself and get in touch with your own feelings, 1st position is a good position to adopt when initially setting outcomes for yourself. It is a position from which to ask yourself the question 'What do I really want?' It is also an appropriate position in which to do an ecology check for any outcomes you set yourself, i.e. does this outcome fit with who I am/want to be? Developing your ability to experience 1st position can be a way of moving from non-assertive to assertive behaviour.

2nd Position   When you can't understand the behaviour of another person, 2nd position is a way of getting behind their behaviour and into their experience and feelings. Once you understand or seek to understand (because there will be times when you cannot absolutely check out that you are right), this will communicate itself to the other person and will often give them a feeling of reassurance that you do understand their position. More especially, it will give you greater understanding and therefore choice about how to deal with the situation taking into account how the other person is affected by it.

3rd Position   This position can be valuable when you want to stand back, take stock and think objectively about a situation. It can be particularly valuable when you don't want the emotions attached to either being in or thinking about a situation. People who are able to handle aggression from others in a controlled and unemotional way often do this from 3rd position so that they are not, for example, experiencing the feelings of anger, frustration or hurt that they might be feeling if they were in 1st position.

IN BLOCKED SITUATIONS

If you want still further choices in a situation when there is conflict or blocks to making progress, then step into the presupposition 'Behind every behaviour is a positive intention towards you'. This is one of the beliefs of excellence explained in Chapter 2.1.

This does not have to be true. You only have to think and act as if it were true. Some creativity helps here in your thinking about what the positive benefit might be. What is the potential benefit in the situation for you? How can you turn the situation into an opportunity even though it may not have initially presented itself to you in this way? For example, if you are faced with someone who is asking you awkward questions, they may be doing that to test the validity of your ideas so that they can decide whether to use them or not. That is a reason for them to ask questions for themselves. However, a benefit for you may be to provide you with the opportunity of learning how to deal with awkward questions and thereby improve your skills as a presenter.

EXAMPLES OF BENEFITS

A manager speaks to you in a way that you find rude and demotivating.

To show you what managerial behaviour doesn't work, so that when you are in a leadership role you know which behaviours to use and which ones to avoid.

A colleague fails to understand a point you are making in a meeting. No matter how much you explain they still say, 'It doesn't make sense.'

For you to demonstrate the real understanding and patience that you would like them to show to you. Also for you to develop even greater flexibility in the way you put your points across.

In the scenario involving James earlier in this section, his ability to adopt different perceptual positions and to consider the positive intention behind his manager's behaviour will affect his response to the situation.

James was experiencing the situation with his manager from a dominant 1st position. When James did eventually step into

2nd position, i.e. he put himself into his manager's shoes, he experienced a strong feeling of insecurity and perceived the ideas being presented to him by James as a threat to his position. James (in 1st position) had never realised this possibility and was shocked to realise how his manager might be feeling. When James considered the situation objectively from 3rd position, he realised that the more that the James in 1st position pushed and initiated new ideas, the more his manager resisted and blocked him. By continuing to do more of the same he was intensifying the response he received.

And the benefit to James of his manager's behaviour? (Remember this does not have to be true. He only has to act as if it were.) It could be that:

- he wants James to learn how to show real empathy towards someone else;

- he is helping James to learn how to approach solutions at a slower pace than he has done previously;

- he wants James to prioritise and think through his ideas so that he only puts over the ones that are of the highest importance to everyone;

- he wants James to develop 2nd position thinking!

When James re-evaluated the situation having experienced it in 1st, 2nd and 3rd positions, he decided to take a different approach to the next meeting. He took more of a back seat initially and supported the ideas that his manager put forward. He waited until his manager asked him for an idea before volunteering any, and he explained what support he would need for the idea to work. He invited his manager to develop the idea further. He regularly checked out how he thought his manager might be feeling as he did this. Over time he gained more and more of his manager's support. Eventually he was able to put forward his ideas without waiting to be asked and he and his manager worked together more cohesively as a team than they had ever done before. When James' manager was appointed to the position of Director of Special Projects he invited James to join him in the new department as Senior Project Manager.

ORGANISATIONAL IMPLICATIONS

Similarly to individuals, companies operate from different positions.

IMPLICATIONS OF COMPANIES OPERATING PRIMARILY FROM ONE POSITION

1st Position   There may be a fire-fighting, crisis management style. The company may jump to conclusions about what the solutions to problems might be without checking that they are the solutions in, say, their customers' minds.
They are more likely to be problem oriented rather than solution oriented because they don't stand back, take stock and consider situations objectively.

or

2nd Position   The company may 'go overboard' to do what the customer wants and asks for, without seeking to influence the solution or the outcome. Even though they may 'jump' to the customer's requests, this may in fact lose the customer's respect for them as an organisation, especially if they don't say what is important to them as a company and promise unrealistic results just to keep the customer happy in the short term.

or

3rd Position   This company stays emotionally detached. This is characteristic of some large, bureaucratic organisations where there is no 'personal touch'. Correspondence will be written in the third person, rarely signed by identifiable individuals. It is difficult to attach accountability to anyone in particular.

CHARACTERISTICS OF A COMPANY THAT TAKES ALL PERCEPTUAL POSITIONS

1st Position   It has a clear mission statement that provides direction for all its employees.
It has agreed, published values that everyone in the company believes in and

lives to on a day by day basis.

Employees have personal development and work outcomes to which they are committed.

and

2nd Position   Employees spend time with their customers (internal and external), finding out their true requirements and collecting regular feedback about how they are doing.

They listen to what their customers have to say.

and

3rd Position   Individuals and teams take time to stand back, take stock and review how they are doing.

They pay attention to process as well as content.

They learn from experience so that they ensure they are on a track of continuous improvement.

TAKING A BALANCED POSITION ON ASSERTION

Assertion is the ability to stand up for your needs and desires in a way that takes account of other people's needs and desires. This is a process of cooperation that leads to an increased likelihood of a win/win outcome. We know from the principles of outcome thinking, explained in Chapter 2.2, that 'dovetailing' outcomes in this way increases the chances that you will achieve what you want. So assertion is about balance, balance between yourself and others.

Achieving win/win

Many of the books and training about assertion teach phrases to use and body language to adopt. They teach behavioural solutions. The work done by Ken and Kate Back on assertiveness, however, addresses beliefs and thinking patterns as ways of becoming more assertive. NLP research has shown us that for meaningful and lasting change to occur, it is important to understand the implications for identity, beliefs, values, capabilities and environment as well as behaviour. For example, it is pointless teaching someone to behave assertively if they believe that aggression is the way to get on in business. So the logical levels model, explained in Chapter 2.6, offers us insight about the different levels that need to be addressed.

Managing the thinking process

In my experience, one of the pieces that makes the biggest difference in enabling people to be more assertive is the ability to manage the thinking process. If you are thinking how difficult it will be to negotiate a good deal with your customer, then it is unlikely that you will handle the situation confidently. Your thinking will influence the outcome. The use of perceptual positions and thinking patterns is in my view the most powerful route to developing assertive ways of thinking and behaving.

Dawn was considered by her colleagues to behave aggressively in many everyday situations. Typically, she would promote her own ideas and plans without consulting others. She felt that her own ideas were generally more appropriate and worthwhile compared with the ideas of her colleagues. She often got frustrated with others but was generally unconcerned.

When Dawn explored the patterns of her thinking about these situations she realised that she was outside herself (dissociated). However, it was as though she was somewhere on the ceiling looking down on the situation. She also noticed that she was much closer to herself in her imagination than she was to others. Although she could see the others and she could see them moving their lips as if they were speaking, she couldn't hear any words.

Dawn experimented with her thinking. First of all she changed her position in her thinking so that she was at eye level with the people in her remembered situation. She also made herself equidistant from herself and the other people. She then associated into her picture of herself so that she could see the situation as if from her own eyes, hear it from her own ears and experience the feelings of being there. Eventually as Dawn brought this balance into her thinking she began to notice that she brought a greater balance into the way she handled situations.

Pauline had felt very stressed for several months. She was concerned about her son, who she believed was sometimes being bullied at school. She was also concerned about her mother who had been ill for some time. She herself had recently taken on a lot more responsibility at work. The result of this was that she was constantly feeling tired and depressed.

When Pauline described how she thought about these situations she invariably saw the situation either as if she were in the other person's shoes, or sometimes if she was dissociated she would be close to the other person. Even in this dissociated state she experienced feelings and she discovered that the feelings were not her own but those of the other person. There was no place in her thinking where she was free of emotion and not surprisingly she felt unable to think about these situations objectively. She was weighed down with everyone's feelings most of the time.

Pauline discovered that by stepping out of 2nd position and giving back the feelings to the rightful owner she began to feel more relaxed (more like herself again!). She positioned herself so that she was equidistant from herself and the other person in her thinking; she effectively started to take a more balanced view of the situation. She began to be able to handle the situations more objectively.

Giving back feelings

Your thinking patterns are the template for your experience. If your thinking about a situation is out of balance then you will probably find yourself giving one part of the situation or one person a greater priority than others. Typically, non-assertive behaviour results from giving others a higher priority than you give yourself. Aggressive behaviour results from giving yourself a higher priority than those around you. Excessive use of 1st position thinking can result in aggressive behaviour. Excessive use of 2nd position thinking can lead to non-assertive behaviour.

Similarly the balance, or lack of it, in your thinking about the situation will influence your level of assertion. If you imagine other people as larger than life with booming voices and yourself as small with a quiet, squeaky voice, then it is not surprising to find yourself responding non-assertively.

However, the difference in using NLP techniques to achieve assertion compared with more traditional approaches is that by changing your thinking process you will find your own words and phrases. You will discover your own assertive non-verbal behaviour. NLP gives you the space to discover your own solutions, styles that fit with who you are and who you want to be. It assumes that you already have all the resources you need to achieve what you want. NLP is a process that enables you to draw on these resources when and where you want them.

STEP ASIDE FROM EMOTION

There are times when it can be useful to detach yourself from the emotion. This is when 3rd position thinking can be valuable. Have you ever witnessed someone else on the receiving end of feedback and known that it was just what they needed to hear — yet you've seen them block the feedback in some way? It can often seem so much easier when you're on the outside, a third party so to speak. This is what many people do who are able to receive feedback effectively.

Receiving feedback

Imagine you have been in a meeting, where you have been presenting your ideas for the way forward on a new project. You have had to push your ideas hard because you feel that your colleagues can be slow to make decisions and the completion of this project is important to your personal success in the company. When the meeting is over one of your colleagues comes up and says, 'You certainly came over aggressively then. You just succeeded in getting several people's backs up.'

How would you feel? How would you respond? There are two very characteristic ways of replying. One would be to attack: 'Well, if you lot were prepared to make a decision once in a while, maybe I wouldn't have to push so hard.'

The other is to defend: 'I didn't think that was aggressive. I was just ensuring my ideas got a response.'

What happens to lead us to do either of these? When someone gives you feedback, they are usually giving you their own or someone else's perception of you. The key point then is whether that perception matches your own or is different.

If it is the same then there usually isn't a problem for most people. If it is different, this is when there is more likely to be an attacking or a defensive response.

In a way the other person's perception of you is a challenge to your own perception. To take it on board would mean to change or extend your perception of yourself in some way. Are you willing to do that? What does it take to do that? Feedback can be a challenge to what is familiar to you, to your comfort zone.

Seeing it through your own eyes and re-experiencing the feedback as if you were there is 1st position thinking. This is where you experience feelings, emotions. It is more likely that if you experience situations from this 1st position you will respond with feelings. If the feelings are strong they can block your ability to take in what others are saying to you.

If you step into the shoes of the giver of the feedback, you may begin to understand their motives and feelings in giving you feedback. And if you experience it as if you were an observer (3rd position thinking) then it really is as if you are outside the situation, experiencing it in a detached way. This is the place where you may find it easier to understand and open your mind to the feedback.

SUMMARY

Perceptual positions are an elegant and powerful way of creating choice and understanding in situations that might otherwise be blocked. The ability to take on different positions is a way of stepping beyond the limitations of everyday behaviour and appreciating the different maps of the world from which we all operate. It is a way of understanding situations from others' perspectives. It is also a way of removing yourself from the emotions of a situation when you need to be able to think in a more detached and objective way about what is going on. And it is a way of getting in touch with your own feelings and desires.

The balanced use of these positions, either as an individual or as a company, gives you flexibility and an increased chance of achieving a win/win outcome to which all parties are committed.

THOUGHT PROVOKERS

1   What could be the positive intention towards you of the following behaviours:

   a   Your manager refuses to let you take on the extra responsibility you have requested.

   b   A colleague appears not to listen to what you have to say.

   c   The senior management team in your company reorganises the structure of the company just as you were beginning to feel settled and secure.

   d   The company you have applied to for a job turns you down.

   e   A colleague in another department fails to respond to your requests for the information you need.

2   From which position (1st, 2nd or 3rd) do you think
     each of these people is operating:

a   Peter was explaining to his team what he wanted
     from them. When the team members didn't
     understand he became frustrated and started to
     explain again in more detail. He felt that although
     he had put forward ideas that would undoubtedly
     benefit them in the long term, they were being
     unreasonable by not appreciating what he meant.
     He found the whole process depressing and
     decided to continue with it anyway without
     consultation as he knew they would appreciate
     it in the end.

b   Jenny was a member of a project team. The success
     of the project was crucial for the company and the
     team often worked late and intensely to achieve
     the deadlines. Often the discussion in these late
     night sessions would become quite heated. Jenny
     stayed calm and couldn't always understand why
     the other members of the team got so upset.
     Sometimes they would get frustrated with her and
     accuse her of not caring about the project. She
     knew that she did, however, and was often able to
     help reconcile different points of view within the
     team.

c   Diane was considered to be a caring manager. She
     always took account of the feelings of her team.
     She was cautious about change, however,
     particularly changes that would upset anyone.
     She was always available to counsel friends and
     colleagues but found that she would take on their
     feelings and often ended the day feeling upset and
     depressed, even though she knew that she had
     helped her colleagues by listening to them.

3   In what situation do you operate primarily with:

●   the person closest to you?

●   your colleagues?

●   your boss?

●   the different members of your family?

A father and his son owned a farm. They did not have many animals but they did own one horse. One day the horse ran away.

'How terrible, what bad luck,' said the neighbours.

'Good luck, bad luck, who knows?' replied the farmer.

Several weeks later the horse returned, bringing with him four wild mares.

'What marvellous luck,' said the neighbours.

'Good luck, bad luck, who knows?' said the farmer.

The son began to learn to ride the wild horses, but one day he was thrown and broke his leg.

'What bad luck,' said the neighbours.

'Good luck, bad luck, who knows?' replied the farmer.

The next week the army came to the village to take all the young men to war. The farmer's son was still disabled with his broken leg so he was spared. Good luck, bad luck, who knows?

2.5 Tap into the Resources You Want — Anchors

When managing change for yourself or facilitating it for others, one of the challenges is to hold onto the changes and the emotions that you generate along the way. Anchoring is a way of doing this. An anchor is a stimulus, it may be a sound, an image, a touch, a smell or a taste, that triggers a consistent response in you or someone else.

The ability to use anchors in NLP enables you to:

- access the resources (feelings and states) that you want when you want them;

- replace unwanted feelings and thoughts with desirable ones;

- gain control over your emotions;

- influence the response you trigger in other people;

- tap into memory and imagination when you want to as part of your personal development.

You already have anchors that work for you. It is likely that you will also have anchors that are currently counterproductive in nature.

For example, think of the associations you have with:

- your favourite piece of music;

- a special perfume;

- a specific touch;

- the taste of a memorable meal;

- a view of a special place.

Any one of these may automatically trigger another memory or emotion; they are linked together. The question is, are the triggered responses the ones you want?

Triggers

I was watching a presentation given as part of a day's assessment for a management training job. The candidate's flipcharts had just disappeared in a heap over the back of the flipchart stand. His response was, 'Beam me up Scottie!' His humour was appreciated by the panel of assessors and the candidate was able to collect his flipcharts and proceed confidently with the presentation.

With those four words he had been able to transform the situation in which he found himself. With those same words and a push of the transmitter button, Captain Kirk and any of his crew were able to 'beam up' to the *Starship Enterprise*. Have you ever wondered what it would be like to be able to do that whenever you chose, to transport yourself from one place to another at the push of a button?

Well, the fact is that you already do this. The question is whether the place you transport yourself to is the place you really want to be. What if Captain Kirk when pushing the button found himself not on the *Enterprise* but on the enemy Klingon warship instead? Read on and you will discover how to choose the destination you want and be sure to get there.

Choosing your response

MAKING ANCHORS WORK FOR YOU

Sometimes people use anchors in a way that triggers unresourceful states, such as depression, anger or frustration. These are states that typically limit your subsequent behavioural choices. Take, for example, someone who consistently becomes depressed. You might ask, 'How do you get that way?' This is a far more useful question than, 'Why do you feel this way?' as it raises awareness of the structure of the experience as opposed to reinforcing the reasons for the state and consequently the state itself. 'I keep telling myself what a

How, not why

mess I've made of my life,' they reply. 'That's how you do it!' It is interesting how skilled some people become at generating unresourceful states for themselves.

Working with a manufacturing company we were invited to explore the staff's resistance to the new appraisal scheme. We discovered that previously the only time a manager typically sat down with a member of his or her staff was when they perceived a problem. Any discussion between a manager and a member of their staff was usually a critical one. It was no surprise then to understand that the staff would be reluctant to welcome any scheme that promoted a discussion with their manager! The managers were unwittingly linking (anchoring) discussions about problems with the appraisal scheme.

By using anchors in conjunction with outcome thinking you begin to take control of the effect you have on yourself and others. For example, you can decide first of all how you want to feel in key situations such as:

Taking control

- at the start of a presentation;

- on the receiving end of aggression;

- when you are about to tell someone they have been made redundant;

- when delegating an area of work to a new employee for the first time;

- in a meeting when your point of view is different to that of the majority;

- when your boss gives you some tough feedback.

Similarly you can decide what effect you want to have on other people, for example:

- when they are entering a discussion with you;

- when you are delegating jobs to them;

- when they have feedback to give to you;

- when you are asking them for a decision.

You have the ability to influence your own and others' responses in a way that is resourceful, i.e. one in which you have confidence and choice about what you can do.

ANCHORING A RESOURCEFUL STATE FOR YOURSELF

Let's start by considering how to generate for yourself the state that you want. The process of anchoring involves linking a specific sight, sound or touch with an experience that is present, i.e. a situation into which you are 'associated'. This linking process subsequently enables you to use the anchor to re-access that same experience.

PROCEDURE FOR ANCHORING A RESOURCEFUL STATE FOR YOURSELF

1   Choose a place that is free from distractions and make yourself comfortable.

2   Decide on a state/a feeling that you have experienced in your life that you would like to be able to access when you choose.

3   Choose an anchor that you can use whenever you want to access this feeling. It must be something precise and easy to use. For example, you could use the little finger and thumb together on your left hand.

4   Now recall the memory of a time when this feeling was at its strongest for you. Check that you are associated into this experience, that you are seeing it as if through your own eyes and not as if you are an observer watching yourself. If you can see yourself in the picture as opposed to seeing it through your own eyes you are dissociated. It is only in the associated state that you can really experience the feelings and therefore anchor them. The concept of association/dissociation is explained in Chapter 1.2.

When you are completely associated, when you are there, pay attention to what you see. What colours can you see? Are they bright or pastel? Is it clear or hazy? Notice the quality of what you see and any other distinctions. What do you hear? Is it loud or quiet? What is the location of the sounds? Are there voices, are you speaking to other people? Listen to those sounds and anything else you hear. As you see this scene, allow yourself to experience the feeling of being there until that feeling is strong and enveloping for you. As you do so, touch your little finger and thumb together for as long and only as long as you feel these sensations intensely. When you have experienced the feeling and the touch of your finger to thumb, release that touch. Shake yourself or move in some way so that you bring yourself back to the present, which is called breaking state.

5   This touch has become the anchor for the feelings. Repeat the process several times until you know that there is a strong connection between the touch and the feelings.

6   Test the anchor. Think of something else and as you do so touch your little finger and thumb together in precisely the way you did it when you were setting up the anchor. This is called firing the anchor.

What happens?

If you have set up the anchor effectively you will recall the scene, the sounds and the feelings of the memory as if you are there.

If this doesn't happen, keep practising. It may be you weren't fully associated when you set the anchor. Check that you use exactly the same anchor to recall the experience as you used to set it up in the first place.

The sensations in an experience tend to rise and fade. Set the anchor just as the experience is reaching a peak, and remove it as soon as or just before the feelings begin to fade.

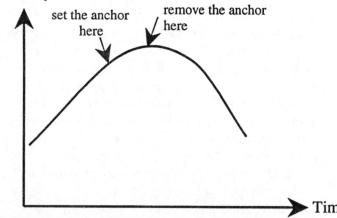

> 7   Now think of a future situation where you would like
>   to have these feelings that you have anchored. This
>   time as you imagine the situation in the future, fire
>   the anchor. What do you see, hear and feel now?
>   When you do this successfully you are transferring
>   your desired feelings, your resourceful state, to
>   another and in this case future context.

Learn first to do this for yourself so that you can recall the
resources you want when you want them.

Remember the key factors in anchoring:

- Fully associate into the experience before you set the
  anchor.

- Make the anchored experience intense.

- Use a distinct and specific anchor that is easily
  reproduced.

- Set the anchor just prior to reaching the most intense
  part of the experience.

- Use exactly the same anchor to recall the experience.

In this example we used a touch as an anchor, but an anchor
can be anything as long as it meets the criteria above.

TAKE RESPONSIBILITY FOR YOUR EFFECTS ON OTHERS

Exactly the same process works for anchoring others as it does
for yourself. You cannot always easily know exactly when the
point of greatest intensity has occurred for someone else in
order to know when to set the anchor. You rely on your ability
to detect from their external behaviour exactly when this
occurs. By building rapport and taking a 2nd position with
them you will learn to detect when this peak state is occurring.
Otherwise the process is exactly the same as it would be if you
were anchoring yourself.

STEPS FOR ANCHORING OTHERS

> I   Ask the other person what state they want to have in
>   a particular situation. Ask them to identify a time in
>   the past when they had that state.

2   Decide on the anchor you are going to use and get yourself positioned so that you can use it easily.

3   Ask the other person to step into that time when they had the state they want now. Help them to associate fully into that experience by asking them about the quality of what they see, hear and feel. Use present tense questions to encourage them to associate into the experience, e.g. 'What do you see?', 'What do you hear?', 'What are your feelings?'

4   Invite them to experience fully all the sensations of being there so that they intensify the experience. Do this by exploring with them each of their senses in this experience, visual, auditory, feelings.

5   Pay attention to them so that when you know that they are reaching the peak of that experience, apply the anchor. Apply it for as long as they experience the feeling intensely.

6   As soon as the intensity of the feelings begins to diminish (again you need to calibrate them to establish when this occurs), stop applying the anchor and bring them back to the present. You can repeat these steps a few times if you want to ensure that the anchor and the state are associated.

7   Test by applying (firing) the anchor. If the anchor works you will see the person reproduce all the external behaviours of the state once again. If this doesn't happen, go back and repeat the process, checking for full association, intensity of the experience and accuracy of the anchor.

8   Now test the anchor in a future situation. Ask the other person to identify a future situation in which they want to have this anchored state. Ask them to imagine that future situation and as they do that fire the anchor. Watch what happens. If the anchor works you will see them manifest the same external responses to the anchor in this future situation.
    Eventually what happens is that they will be able to think of the future situation and get the state automatically without having to fire the anchor.

You are anchoring other people all the time. The question is, are you anchoring them in resourceful or unresourceful ways?

In a company I worked for some years ago, we had a team meeting every Friday afternoon. This unfortunately was when most of the team felt at their most tired, but it was the only time when we could all get together. Naturally, most of the team wanted to make decisions quickly so that we could leave early and go home. Harry, one of the team members, often had very creative and constructive ideas. However, when he started to speak, he would raise a difficulty with what had just been discussed. This was a consistent pattern for him. The result was that virtually each time he opened his mouth the rest of the team seemed to inwardly groan and usually ignored or attempted to quash the point he was making. Harry had effectively anchored this response just by opening his mouth!

Can you imagine how different performance appraisals would be if managers were measured by the state in which they left their staff at the end of the discussion?

The examples of anchoring we used earlier in this section, e.g. touch, aren't so available in a business setting. It isn't always part of the culture to touch others in this way. It becomes necessary to become a little more creative with the anchors you use to enable others to access resourceful states.

Examples of anchors you can use in business are:

BUSINESS ANCHORS

- A word or words that you would not use regularly in conversation, said with a specific volume and tonality.

- Use of space. This can be used to good effect in a presentation where you can anchor different information and responses to you by standing or moving to different parts of the room.

- A posture or movement that you would not naturally make in discussion.

My experience is that using anchors in this way only works if you use them with integrity, i.e. in a way that fits with other people's outcomes. I believe that if you attempt to use them in a manipulative way, i.e. in a way that is out of line with the other person's outcomes, then that other person will sense this, often intuitively, and they will subsequently block it.

STEPS FOR ANCHORING A RESOURCEFUL STATE IN A MEETING

1   Identify the state you want to anchor in the other person that will support the achievement of your mutual outcomes. This might, for example, be a state of confidence, decisiveness or happiness.

2   Decide what anchor you will use, a particular word or a specific gesture or posture.

3   When the other person naturally demonstrates the desired state, use your anchor. You will probably need to do this four or five times.

4   If the discussion gets to a stage when this state would be valuable and is not naturally occurring, fire your anchor. Notice what happens.

SWITCHING STATES

There are many different ways of using anchors. One easy way is to use a technique called **collapsing anchors**. This is a way of reconciling two states, for example an unresourceful state and a resourceful one.

One of the simplest ways to do this is to use the knuckles on one hand. With the extreme end of your right-hand index finger you are going to touch specific knuckles on your left hand. If it is easier for you, reverse the way you use your hands in this exercise.

STEPS FOR COLLAPSING ANCHORS

1   Decide on an unresourceful state you want to work with in this exercise. It might be, for example, a state of anxiety, stress, lack of confidence or frustration.

2   Associate into this state so that you are re-experiencing it and anchor it by touching your index finger to the first knuckle on the other hand. Test the anchor until you know it works. Only access this state briefly.

3   Choose a different state altogether, a break state. This might be thinking about something funny or just

something that requires some thought, like saying your phone number backwards.

4   Choose a resourceful state, one of confidence, calm or security, for example. Associate into a time when you had this feeling. When you experience the intensity of this feeling, anchor it by touching your second finger to the second knuckle on your other hand.

5   Test the anchors in the following sequence:
    a   Break state.
    b   Fire the first anchor.
    c   Break state.
    d   Fire the second anchor.
        If either of the anchors fails to work, repeat the sequence of resetting them.

6   Now apply both anchors simultaneously. You will feel some confusion as the two states sort themselves out into a new, integrated state. If the less resourceful state is still a strong part of the subsequent state, go back and choose and anchor an even stronger resourceful state. Repeat the process. You may also find it helps to fire the anchor for the resourceful state a second or two before also firing the anchor for the unresourceful state.

7   Now think of a future situation, one which typically in the past would have triggered off the unresourceful state. What happens as you think of this situation? If the collapsing anchors has worked, the unresourceful state will not exist any more.

Some of these techniques may seem quite formal at first. However, once you master the skill, you can begin to use it more informally. For example, if you find yourself slipping into a state of unresourcefulness, you can learn to step quickly into a resourceful one. Recall a time when you felt particularly resourceful and re-access those feelings by associating yourself once more into that situation. Eventually you will find that even the process of switching from unresourceful to resourceful becomes automatic. Your unconscious mind makes the switch

Hard-wiring the strategy

for you without you even having to think about it consciously. You will have 'hard-wired' the strategy for resourcefulness by learning to chain anchors.

I believe that putting yourself into a resourceful state is a vital precursor to most situations. You can learn to recognise which state is most useful to you, for example in:

- giving and receiving feedback;

- solving problems and being creative;

- being assertive;

- listening;

- tackling work that you would not naturally be motivated to do;

- spending time with your family;

- making a presentation;

- dealing with customers.

The list is endless. More traditional training will teach you what structure to use, e.g. how to structure appraisal, how to handle objections. NLP teaches you how to generate the state that triggers the resources and style that you need to achieve what you want.

ANCHORING 'INSIGHT'

One of the characteristics of NLP is that it can accelerate your ability to learn. NLP is about how to manage change skilfully and powerfully. If you can manage and facilitate change you can learn.

Accelerating learning

One of the gifts I was given early in my NLP training was the gift of insight. Insight is the 'a-ha' of the learning process, a realisation, a new connection made or re-realised. I thank my first NLP tutor, Gene Early, for this gift. This is not to say that I didn't have the power of insight previously, but Gene brought it to my conscious awareness and gave me much more access to it as a resource to myself. He did this through anchoring. Gene has an amazing ability to teach to a large group of delegates as if he were talking to each person individually. As he is talking to one person he makes a meaningful glance at another and then another. He often uses glances as anchors.

During a session one day he was engaged in conversation with one of the course members and he turned to me, looked at me directly and said, 'Sue is getting insight as to what this means for her.' Now, whether I actually was or not, the effect of this was that I consciously searched for what that insight might be. Sure enough I got it. In subsequent sessions from time to time Gene gave me that same look, initially with some words about insight but eventually the glance alone had the same effect. Of course, I never knew when I was going to get 'the glance' and it didn't matter. He had set up an anchor so that whenever anyone spoke or indeed whenever anything occurred, I was ready with an insight.

Eventually I no longer needed the glance, the insight had become anchored to everyday experience.

SUMMARY

Anchors are a natural occurrence. You have many associations already established, some individual, some connected with other people. Most of these will have occurred by chance without any forethought. Some of these association-anchors will be helpful, supportive and enjoyable for you. Some will not. The process of anchoring enables you to choose the associations you want both for yourself and for your ability to influence other people. Mastering the skill of anchoring means taking responsibility for managing your own state of mind. It also means taking responsibility for the effect you have on other people.

This chapter has set out a few of the ways in which you can apply the anchoring techniques, but you will find that anchoring is a part of everything you do. Begin to explore how you can use these anchors creatively as a way of enriching your day to day living and as a way of making your involvement with others a rewarding experience.

Anchoring as a way of life

THOUGHT PROVOKERS

1 What state do you typically have in the following
   situations and what state would you like to have?

Situation	Current State	Wanted State
Giving a presentation		
Saying what you want		
Refusing personal requests		
Appraising or being appraised		
Going for an interview		
Exercising		
Dealing with aggression		
Having your ideas challenged in public		

Choose one of the above situations and use either the
self-anchoring or the collapsing anchors technique.

2 Write down the state that you would like to generate
   in yourself and in others in the following situations.

Situation	Own state	Desired state in others
Appraising others		
Giving feedback		
Explaining what you want		
Clarifying technical information		
Running or contributing to meetings		

Use either of the anchoring techniques to experiment
with generating a desired state in yourself and in others.

3   Write down the state that you would like to have when
     dealing with each of the following people and the
     state you would like them to have.

Person	Your desired state	Desired state for them
A member of staff		
A colleague		
Someone in your family		
Your best friend		
A friend		
A customer		
A supplier		

Use either of the anchoring techniques to experiment
with achieving these desired states.

4   Develop a list of anchors that you could use in your
     everyday situations. Check that they meet the outline
     for an effective anchor, i.e. that it is precise and
     easily reproducible, and that it can be used uniquely
     to anchor a specific resource.

Many years ago there was a sailor who had sailed to many different countries around the world. He had been to many places and seen many different sights. One day as he was sailing across the seas he came upon an island and decided to rest there for a while. He moored his boat on the shore and began to look around. All around the island was a beautiful white beach and behind the beach was dense tropical jungle. All was quiet until...

He thought he could hear a faint noise in the distance and tilted his head to listen. He sensed it came from within the jungle and walked closer. Sure enough, once again he heard this faint noise in the background. He started to hack his way through the foliage in order to make a pathway. The more he moved inland the louder the noise became. He continued to cut his way through until eventually he reached a clearing and there in the middle of the clearing he saw an old man sitting cross-legged on the ground.

The old man had his eyes closed and was chanting 'Mo, Mo, Mo' in long, soft tones. The sailor stood and watched and listened. 'Mo, Mo, Mo,' continued the old man. Eventually the sailor approached the old man and tapped him on the shoulder. The old man turned slowly around and smiled.

'Excuse me,' said the sailor, 'I think you have made a mistake. I think you should be saying "Om, Om, Om".'

'Oh,' said the old man smiling. 'Thank you so much,' and began to chant 'Om, Om, Om.'

The sailor felt pleased with himself and made his way back to his boat. He launched his boat again and began to sail away, and when he had sailed for a while he felt a tap on his shoulder. He turned round, surprised to see the old man who said, 'Forgive me for interrupting your journey. Could you please remind me what the chant should be?'

The sailor, still in a state of shock, said, 'Mo, Mo, Mo.'

'Thank you so much,' said the old man and walked back across the water to the island.

Logical Levels of Change 2.6

One of the aims of NLP training and consultancy is personal congruence. By setting compelling outcomes, resolving inner conflict and managing personal change, you can move increasingly towards a state of alignment. This is a focused state in which your energies are harnessed to pull in one direction.

Just as a company can work more effectively if each of the teams within it cooperates and works towards the same goal, so an individual can function more effectively if each of the 'parts' is cooperating with the others. This kind of aligned state can only be achieved if change is dealt with at a number of levels.

Robert Dilts, one of the leading international NLP trainers, has developed a model for change that was originated by Gregory Bateson, the anthropologist. This model, the logical levels of change, provides a useful framework for deciding at what level to work to bring about the required change.

This is the model:

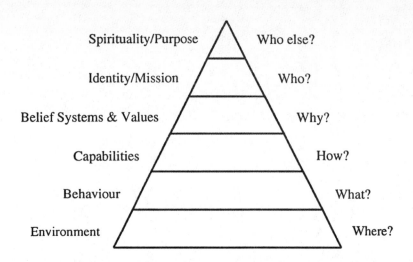

The levels have similar meanings for both individuals and companies alike.

PURPOSE

The level of purpose is sometimes described as the level of spirituality. Although this term can have a religious connotation, this is not its only meaning here. Spiritual refers to the larger system of which you are a part. Understanding the spiritual level for yourself means understanding the interconnections between you and the bigger system and their implications.

This is particularly important for companies. In modelling companies who have achieved long-term success and who are able to develop and grow, we discover that one of the characteristics that sets them apart is their attention to the system of which they are a part. They are companies who have missions that are ecological, i.e. they cooperate and contribute to the bigger system. For example, if it were a travel company it would be one that pays attention to the effect it has on the culture of the countries with which it does business. If it were an information technology company it would be one that had thought about and planned the impact it would have on the future culture and world at large through its development of technology.

IDENTITY/MISSION

The level of identity/mission contains statements that describe how you think of yourself as a person, 'I am' statements, such as:

- 'I am a successful person.'

- 'I am an optimist.'

- 'I am a shy person.'

- 'I am practical.'

For a company the mission statement defines the identity of the organisation, the unique nature of its business. For example:

> Our mission is to support and develop the leaders of today and those destined to be the leaders of tomorrow.

The level of belief systems and values contains statements about yourself, other people and situations that you hold to be true. They are emotionally held views not based on fact:

BELIEF SYSTEMS AND VALUES

- 'I believe that people in general can be trusted.'

- 'I believe that I can learn from any experience I have.'

- 'I believe that the customer's needs are the heart of business success.'

For a company these would be the beliefs on which the company and the way it goes about its business are founded. They only function as beliefs if the everyday behaviour of the management and the employees are an expression of these beliefs. For this to be the case the beliefs need to be ones that are drawn from the organisation's actual employees. Ones picked from a textbook on management because they sound, look or feel good won't work and are more likely to lead to increased dissatisfaction if the everyday behaviour contradicts the published beliefs. However, where they do match, the result can be a major contributory factor to the cohesion and congruence of the organisation.

The values are the criteria against which you make decisions. They are qualities that you hold to be important to you in the way you live your life, for example:

Values

- honesty

- openness

- integrity

- fun

For companies the same principles apply for values as those that applied to beliefs. They only function if they are indeed the values of the employees and management of the organisation, i.e. if the covert and overt values are the same. An agreed and meaningful set of values provides a code of practice for how to go about the business. This is especially important in a culture of autonomy and ownership where you want employees to take initiatives and decisions but want to maintain a company style and set of principles.

CAPABILITIES

Capabilities are increasingly becoming known as competencies. They are resources that you have available to you in the form of skills or qualities. For example sensitivity, adaptability, flexibility, outcome thinking. Many of the NLP core skills are designed to develop capabilities or competencies. Many organisations are paying increasing attention to competency based training and development. It is important to recognise that this is only one of the levels of change.

BEHAVIOUR

Behaviour is what you do and say, what you express externally to the world around you. It is the part of you that can be seen and heard by other people. You can think of behaviour as the tip of the iceberg, the part above the surface, whereas purpose, identity, capabilities, beliefs and values are internal thoughts and feelings.

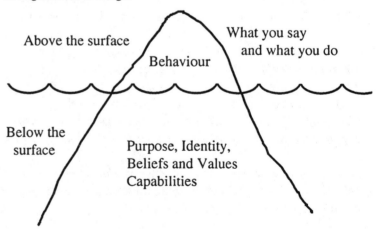

Examples of behaviours:

● asking questions

● saying what you want

- losing your temper

- writing out your goals

- giving feedback

- folding your arms

- smiling

- blushing

- running

- looking at someone

Behaviour can also be reflected in the personal development plans that you set yourself:

- I will set myself priorities every day.

- I will ensure I listen by summarising each meeting I attend.

- I will agree and write up on the flipchart outcomes for each meeting that I hold.

A company has everyday behaviour that is characteristic of the company as a whole or departments and teams within the company. For example:

- The sales support team handles customer queries efficiently and promptly.

- Staff keep you waiting and blame others in the company for any mistakes.

- Employees in the company take initiatives and make decisions on the spot.

It can also be the style of development plans that the company sets itself:

- We will respond to phone calls within three rings.

- We will build quality into everything that we do.

- We will 'empower' people to make their own decisions.

You may have experienced the relative value of the above behavioural plans when they are only set at this level of behaviour: minimal!

ENVIRONMENT

Environment refers to everything 'outside' yourself: the place in which you work, the economy, people around you, your business, your friends and family, your customers. What you think about as being in the environment is also a measure of how much you take responsibility for what happens to you. For example:

- If you say 'It's a tough world out there,' this suggests that you put some of the power and influence outside yourself.

- Equally, talking about 'They...' ('They won't let you...' or 'They don't tell you...'; see Chapter 1.4) gives the same impression.

THE INFLUENCE OF THE LEVELS

Gregory Bateson pointed out that in the processes of learning, change and communication there is a natural hierarchy. The rules for changing something on one level are different to those for changing on a lower level. Changing something on a lower level could, but would not necessarily, affect the higher levels. However, changing something on the higher levels would always change things on the lower levels.

Sustainable change

Your thinking about yourself at the higher levels will determine your thinking and behaviour at the lower levels, whereas, for example, your behaviour may or may not influence your beliefs at the higher level. As in the examples of behaviour earlier in the chapter, companies that only pay attention to behaviour when trying to introduce a new culture of quality, for example, find that the change isn't sustainable unless they also address the higher levels of beliefs and values. In order to bring about change it is necessary to work at the level above the one you want to influence.

Characteristically, NLP training works at the higher levels. Many of the change models are to do with beliefs and identity. Although NLP does include teaching of techniques, the emphasis is on the capabilities such as sensitivity and flexibility to make these techniques work. Much NLP work can be done without knowing the content of the problem or the issue in hand. This distinguishes it from many other forms of training. NLP training operates on the philosophy that:

People have within them all the resources they need to achieve what they want.

REACTIVE OR PROACTIVE?

Imagine yourself in the following situation.

You have been working on a new project for your company for the last six months. It is now nearing completion and all the results have been achieved to plan. You believe that the results of this project are an important contribution to the future of the company. You are pleased with the contribution that you personally have made and expect that the launch of this project will boost your promotion prospects. Two weeks before the launch the directors announce a major company reorganisation. They announce that all projects started within the last year are to be put on hold awaiting any further decision by the board. You and the rest of the project team feel very disappointed and disheartened.

Which of the following would you be more likely to do?

- Accept the situation and feel upset.

- Get inwardly annoyed.

- Complain to others around you about the way you have been treated.

- Hope that someone else takes action to change the decision.

- Ask for a meeting with your manager to discuss the decision.

- Accelerate the completion of the project so that you can announce its readiness for launch.

- Leave the company.

What else might you do? Are you reactive or proactive in the way you respond to events in your life? Puppet master or puppet? What is it that distinguishes those who influence their own destiny from those who leave their fate in the hands of others, or to chance?

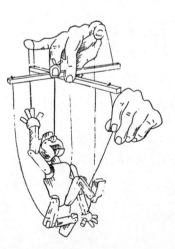

Steve's conversations centred around what he and others do. For example, he would measure the strength of people's friendships towards him in terms of what they would do for him. Equally he expected them to judge the level of his friendship to them by the type of actions he took on their behalf. He was self-employed and considered himself lucky each time a new large contract 'turned up'. He was never entirely sure what the source of the next contract would be. He was influenced a lot by the climate. When the weather was sunny and warm he generally felt more optimistic, whereas when the weather was cold and cloudy he often felt depressed.

Steve is affected by day to day behaviour and the environment. His behaviour is **reactive**.

Attention to lower levels

If your attention is directed mainly to the lower levels of change in Dilts' framework you will be thinking about how you and others behave, in the environment. You will be affected by changes in other people's behaviour and changes in the environment. If the weather is sunny it may cheer you up, if it is dull and wet you feel down. This tends to lead to a more reactive way of dealing with life. A company that concentrates on the lower behavioural and environmental levels will be more likely to respond to 'the competition' rather than moving towards its own vision of the future.

Carla had a very clear sense of identity and mission. She knew what she wanted to achieve and what was important to her. She believed that 'people could be trusted' and that if anyone behaved aggressively towards her it was not meant towards her personally, but was more a statement of what they were feeling inside. She believed that she could learn from whatever happened. She even took times of recession as an opportunity to learn how to approach work and customers differently.

Attention to higher levels

Proactive behaviour requires you to focus on the higher levels of spirituality, mission and identity, beliefs and values. The more able you are to operate independently of other people's behaviour and changes in the environment, the more proactive you become.

'*You carry your own weather around with you.*'
  Stephen Covey, **The Seven Habits of Highly Effective People**

For example, if you believe that people can be trusted, even if someone lets you down it is likely that you will continue to maintain that belief and see the incident as a one-off aberration.

Here are some examples of how different people think about themselves.

A Overall I think I've been very lucky both in my career and in my personal life. I've always been employed and now self-employed, amazingly work always seems to turn up. My personal life has been less smooth and though I have many regrets, especially with regard to my children, I have experienced much happiness. I enjoy being and feeling fit, my work, demonstrating skills that I have and spending time with my kids.

B I am a girl who knows what she wants and how and when I am going to get it. I have decided to become a physiotherapist. I have researched into this and even had some experience in it. This work is right for me and I'm right for it. I'm a happy person who loves helping people. I get along with anyone and everyone, a feature of myself of which I am proud.

C I find it very hard to write about myself, maybe because I am quite a shy and inward person. I don't really like to let people know how I am feeling. I also know that I am a very negative person. I lack confidence in myself so therefore I never believe in what I do. I would like to be more positive in my attitude towards life and I wish I had the ability not to worry and to be more relaxed.

A talks mainly about issues at the level of behaviour and capabilities. This person is more likely to be affected by the behaviour of other people, by situations, by the results he or she achieves. A's style is likely to be reactive. B, on the other hand, discusses herself in terms of her identity. A person who knows what she wants and gets it, a happy person, someone who is proud of herself. This understanding and clarity about her identity will permeate everything she does and the way she perceives her experience.

The writer of C, however, describes himself as a shy and inward person who doesn't believe in what he does and who wishes he could be different. So even though he is sure about his identity, it generates behaviour that he doesn't want and would like to change. It is certain that no matter what others do to tell him he is capable and that he need not worry, his beliefs about his identity will override this.

So the writers of B and C are independently proactive but in quite different ways, whereas the writer of A, whose attention is more at the lower levels, is likely to be significantly affected by day to day changes in behaviour and environment.

Getting a balance

You may be happy as you are. If, however, you are like the subject of C who wants to change, it is important to identify at what level you can make this change. For him the overriding comments were at the level of identity and belief: 'I am quite a shy and inward person,' 'I never believe in what I do.' One does not necessarily have to lead to the other. He could, for example, remain shy and inward and yet believe in what he does. So for him to achieve the changes he wants, he will need to bring about change at the level of identity or spirituality.

For the subject in A, however, it would depend on whether he wanted to change. If he felt he was unduly affected by behaviour and environment and wanted to develop greater independence, then he could pay attention to levels of capabilities, beliefs and identity.

STEPS TO PERSONAL CONGRUENCE

By becoming aware of your thinking at each of these levels you will start to influence the process of personal alignment. The next step is to decide what you want to be true for you at each level. By working your way through the following questions, over time you will begin to develop a sense of personal congruence.

What is the system of which you are a part/would like to influence? In my own case I am a part of the business world. I believe I have a responsibility to that business community to consider the effects of the training that we provide. At a smaller chunk level the training that we give people will influence their relationship with their partners and family. It was in thinking about this that we decided to offer places to the partners of delegates attending our courses so that they could learn together and support each other in that learning. We are also now planning NLP based courses for school and college students.

What is your identity/mission? Thinking about identity and mission can sometimes take months or even years to clarify. Begin by writing down what you think they are. How would you describe yourself? What is your purpose in business, in life?

There are many exercises that can help you to think about this. Some examples are included in the thought provokers at the end of this chapter.

What are your beliefs and values? Be honest with yourself. Write down the beliefs and values that you actually operate to rather than the 'good', textbook words. Think about the decisions that you make on a day by day basis. What are the factors on which you make those decisions? What beliefs do you hold about yourself/other people/your family/your job/your life?

What are your capabilities? Establish your true capabilities. These may be demonstrated not only by what you do in your work but by what you do outside that work. You may not be the best judge of your capabilities. Elicit other people's views on what they might be.

What do you do? What is your everyday behaviour? It is often others who can give this feedback most accurately. Do a self-perception and contrast it with others' perception of how you behave. Identify the behaviours that are characteristic of you, the things you say and the things you do.

What is your environment? Where and when do you do the things identified above? What would you say are the external influences on you and your life?

Just the process of becoming aware of what these things are for you will give you more choice about whether you hold on to them or not. Awareness leads to choice. The person who wrote paragraph C above, describing himself as a shy and inward person, has subsequently experienced significant shifts in his perception of himself. He felt that the process of writing out the paragraph highlighted some of the patterns in his thinking about himself that he didn't like and wanted to change. This person has developed confidence in himself, has been appointed to a position of responsibility and is generally much happier with life and himself.

SUMMARY

Proactivity is one of the fashionable words in business today. And although there is no right and wrong about proactivity and reactivity, there is undoubtedly a trend towards encouraging proactivity in business. The logical levels of change model provides us with a means of understanding the patterns of proactivity and reactivity.

People who are clear about their identity, beliefs and values and whose attention is centred on these levels will be more independent of changes that occur at the levels of behaviour and environment and more proactive in relation to them. People who are less sure of these levels in relation to themselves and whose attention is more at the lower levels will be affected and will react to their own and others' behaviour and changes in the environment.

There are many NLP techniques designed to bring about change at each level and some of these changes may be best brought about with the help of an external facilitator. However, by becoming aware of your thinking and beliefs at each of these levels and by beginning to question and challenge those ones you want to change, you will begin to influence your own personal balance between proactivity and reactivity.

THOUGHT PROVOKERS

1   Consider the following aspects of your life. How close are you in each of these areas to the way you want to be? In the column headed 'Ideal' give each a mark out of 10, where 10 signifies that this is exactly as you want it to be and 0 indicates that it is not at all as you would want it. In the column headed 'Reactive/Proactive' rate yourself in terms of how actively you are influencing each area. 10 indicates you are, in your view, entirely proactive in the way you are influencing this area to bring it up to the ideal. 0 indicates you are waiting and hoping (or you've just given up).

	Ideal 0–10	Reactive/Proactive 0–10
Your job		
Your social life		
Your friends		
Your skills		

You will be building up a picture of where you lie on the reactive–proactive scale. Even if you have what you consider to be an ideal situation, or close to it, you may find that you actively influence that situation to keep it that way.

It can be useful to get other people's feedback on how they perceive you on this scale. It can be easy sometimes to delude yourself, for example into thinking that being busy is the same as being proactive, when in fact what you are doing is having little influence.

2   Take a few moments and imagine you are applying for a new job. Write a paragraph about yourself which, in your view, describes what makes you uniquely you.

3   Ask a colleague or friend if they will answer the following questions in the order given.

a   What do you do?   (*Behaviour*)
b   Where do you do it?   (*Environment*)
c   What skills enable you to do what you do?
                                              (*Capabilities*)
d   What is important to you about what you
     do?   (*Values*)
e   What do you believe is true about you and
     those around you that enables you to do what
     you do?   (*Beliefs*)
f   Who are you?   (*Identity*)
g   Of which systems are you a part?   (*Spirituality*)

How easy did they find it to answer the questions? Was it easier at the beginning or at the end? How did the quality of the communication change as you progressed through the questions? Each question corresponds to one of the logical levels of change. The ease with which your partner answered the questions can be an indication of how familiar that level of thinking about themselves is to them.

Gilbert Kaplan was an American millionaire publisher. He had achieved all the key business goals he had ever set himself. He was also a Mahler enthusiast. His obsession began in 1965, when as a young Wall Street economist he heard Stokowski conduct the Second Symphony. From then on he attended every live performance possible of that symphony, avidly studied every recording and eventually at the age of 40 conceived the wild idea of conducting the work himself. The experts sniffed. Kaplan's only musical training lay in childhood piano lessons.

When he eventually gave his first public performance people came out of curiosity and disbelief. They had heard of his obsession but knew what sort of training it took to develop the ability to conduct and in particular to conduct the music of Mahler. As the performance began Kaplan realised that he could not synchronise his conducting with the sound of the orchestra. He was unfamiliar with the acoustics of the hall. The audience were not surprised, after all it was to be expected. The performance was a failure.

Kaplan, however, was undeterred. He believed in his ability eventually to conduct Mahler. He continued to study. He was particularly obsessed with Mahler's Resurrection Symphony. He memorised this complex score, and travelled to hear the work whenever it was performed. He decided he was ready to give a performance in 1982 and did so with the American Symphony Orchestra. His revealing interpretation confounded the critics and won him worldwide requests to repeat the performance.

Kaplan now devotes his spare time to Mahler research, financing in 1986 a finely documented and superbly produced facsimile of the Resurrection Symphony whose original score he now owns. He has conducted 33 international performances of the symphony.

PART 3

THE TOOLKIT

This toolkit is a selection of questionnaires and exercises designed to help you apply some of the principles of NLP to yourself. For many of the NLP techniques there is no substitute for practical experience and face-to-face training. However, the toolkit is designed to raise your awareness of some of your patterns of thinking and behaving. I hope it will both answer some existing questions you may have and raise some new ones for your unconscious mind to play with.

Identify Your Preferred Thinking Pattern 3.1

Aim: To help you identify your preferred thinking style.
Reference Chapter: 1.1 Thinking Patterns

For each of the following questions, think about the item, person or place described and tick the element(s) that come to mind. Check your answers on the analysis sheet provided at the end of the chapter.

1. Petrol.
   a. An image of some sort, e.g. a car, a petrol station?
   b. A sound, e.g. the sound of petrol pouring into a tank, the sound of an explosion?
   c. A touch, e.g. the feel of the pump handle?
   d. A smell, e.g. the smell of the petrol?
   e. A taste, e.g. the taste of petrol (assuming you know!)?

2. Your best friend.
   a. A sound, e.g. the sound of their voice?
   b. An emotion, e.g. your feelings towards them?
   c. A smell, e.g. the smell of their perfume?
   d. A taste, e.g. the taste of a meal you ate with them?
   e. An image, e.g. what they look like or a place you have been to with them?

3. The way you would most like to spend your time.
   a. The sounds associated with doing this, e.g. the sound of people's voices or the sounds of the environment?
   b. A taste, e.g. the taste of a particular food?
   c. A smell, e.g. the aroma of your environment?

    d.   An image, e.g. where you would be or who you would be with?

    e.   A touch or an emotion, e.g. how you feel when you think of spending your time this way?

4. What you did yesterday.
    a.   A taste of some sort, e.g. what you ate?
    b.   An image or picture, e.g. the scene of where you were?
    c.   A sound or maybe a conversation?
    d.   A touch, sensation or emotion?
    e.   A smell, e.g. of your environment?

5. A time you didn't enjoy very much.
    a.   A smell, e.g. an aroma?
    b.   A sound, e.g. what you heard or what you were saying to yourself?
    c.   A taste?
    d.   An image, e.g. of what was happening or what you could imagine?
    e.   A touch, e.g. the feel of something, or an emotion, e.g. how you felt at that time?

6. Your favourite restaurant.
    a.   A touch or emotion, e.g. how you felt being there?
    b.   What you see, e.g. the people you are with, your surroundings?
    c.   What you hear, e.g. the conversation, the music?
    d.   A taste, e.g. of the food?
    e.   A smell, e.g. the aroma from the kitchen?

7. Something from your early childhood.
    a.   A smell, an aroma, a perfume?
    b.   A touch or an emotion?
    c.   An image?
    d.   Sounds or voices?
    e.   A taste?

8. Your work.
    a.   A sound, e.g. of equipment or voices?
    b.   An image, e.g. the picture of what you do?
    c.   A taste?
    d.   A smell, e.g. of your surroundings?
    e.   A touch or an emotion, e.g. the texture of what you can feel or how you feel about your work?

9. Where you might be tomorrow.
    a.   An image or picture?
    b.   An emotion or touch?
    c.   A taste?
    d.   A smell or aroma?
    e.   A sound?

10. Something you find difficult to do.
    a.   An image or picture?
    b.   A taste?
    c.   A sound or an inner conversation?
    d.   An associated emotion or a touch?
    e.   A smell?

11. Something you find rewarding.
    a.   An emotion, e.g. a feeling of satisfaction, or a
         touch, e.g. the physical sensation of a sport?
    b.   A taste?
    c.   A smell?
    d.   A sound, e.g. what you say to yourself or the
         sound of voices or your environment?
    e.   An image, e.g. of what it looks like?

12. Something you find amusing.
    a.   A sound, e.g. what someone says or what you hear?
    b.   An image, e.g. something or someone you see?
    c.   An emotion, e.g. the sensation of amusement, or
         a physical touch, e.g. the feel of something?
    d.   A taste?
    e.   A smell?

THINKING PATTERNS ANALYSIS

Circle the letters you ticked for each answer.

	Visual	Auditory	Feelings	Taste	Smell
1	a	b	c	e	d
2	e	a	b	d	c
3	d	a	e	b	c
4	b	c	d	a	e
5	d	b	e	c	a
6	b	c	a	d	e
7	c	d	b	e	a
8	b	a	e	c	d
9	a	e	b	c	d
10	a	c	d	b	e
11	e	d	a	b	c
12	b	a	c	d	e

TOTALS

Now add up the number of letters circled in each column. These scores indicate your preferences in thinking patterns, i.e. the higher the score, the more likely you are to use this sense as a way of processing information. There are no right answers.

Receive Feedback Constructively 3.2

Aim: To enable you to receive feedback openly and constructively.
Reference Chapters: 1.1 Thinking Patterns; 1.2 Filters on your World

1. Think of a situation when someone gave you feedback that you had difficulty accepting. Maybe you responded aggressively or possibly defensively. It is a situation where you would like to have had the choice of responding openly and constructively. (You may or may not agree with the feedback given.)

2. As you re-experience that situation, be aware of whether you are 'in your shoes' or outside yourself, able to see and hear yourself as if an observer.

3. If you are not already detached in your thinking, then step outside yourself (dissociate) so that you can see and hear yourself as an observer.

4. Imagine that you are watching yourself on video on a television screen and you now have access to the controls. The controls can change the brightness, the colour and the volume. There are also controls that enable you to change the way the 'you' in the picture feels and responds.

5. Decide how you would like the 'you' on the receiving end of the feedback to respond. What would you like the 'you' there to be able to say and do? What inner resources would the 'you' there need to be able to respond in that way? Would it be self-confidence, relaxation, understanding?

6. Take your time and create the 'you' on the screen that is most able to listen, understand, question and take in the feedback that is appropriate. Remember you have all the controls you need to change the 'you' on the screen.

7. When the 'you' on the screen has these new resources, you can press the play button on the video and watch yourself receiving the feedback from the other person. If at any point you sense the 'you' on the screen blocking the feedback in any way, press the pause button and identify what further resources you need to remain open to what you hear.

8. When the 'you' on the screen is hearing and responding to the feedback in the way that you want, identify a likely future situation where you want to receive feedback in a similar way.

9. Imagine yourself into the situation as if you were there.

10. Repeat steps 4–7 for this future situation.

11. Play it through until you know you can respond in the way you want to respond.

There may be other factors, for example your beliefs, that hinder your ability to accept feedback openly. Nevertheless the technique outlined above is a powerful one and will change your experience of receiving feedback so that it is more in line with how you want it to be.

Identify Your Filters 3.3

Aim: For you to begin to identify the filters you use.
Reference Chapter: 1.2 Filters on your World

Answer the following questions for each area that is relevant to you.

1. Think of yourself exercising. Tick the thoughts that are most like the ones that come to mind.

    Exercise/fitness

    a. Getting fit.
    b. Avoiding injury.
    c. Having a sense of personal achievement.
    d. Losing weight.
    e. Enjoying the environment.
    f. Taking your mind off the pressure of work.

2. When you think of changing your job which of the following are you most likely to think about?

    Changing job

    a. The kind of work you would most like to do.
    b. The situations and people you don't like and want to avoid.
    c. The satisfaction you will get from doing what you want.
    d. The frustrations you experience currently.
    e. The things that your current job doesn't give you.
    f. The kind of work that satisfies your needs.

Going on holiday

3 When you make a decision to go on holiday which of the following do you do?

    a. Think of the problems of organising a holiday.
    b. Begin to imagine yourself there on holiday.
    c. Think of what your holiday will be like.
    d. Remind yourself of all the benefits of taking a holiday.
    e. Think of some of the problems you have experienced on previous holidays.
    f.   Think of everything you have to do first.

Look at the following shapes

4 Write one sentence that explains their relationship to each other.

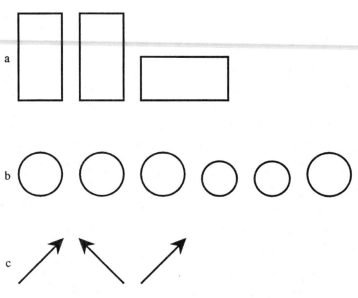

You are buying something

5 It may help to think of something that you are in the process of buying currently — a car, a house, a book, an item of clothing. Which of the following do you do?

    a. Look for aspects of this purchase that are the same as similar purchases you have made before.
    b. Think the purchase through to discover in what ways it doesn't meet your needs.
    c. Compare the purchase with a mental or actual list of characteristics that you want to have.
    d. Search for something that is different to what you have had before.
    e. Seek to find out how this product matches up to similar products.
    f.   Want something that is unique, there is no other like it.

6   In conversation, which of the following applies to you?   *Conversation*

    a.   You like a good argument.
    b.   You look for the common agenda.
    c.   You push for agreement.
    d.   You test out someone else's views to find out where they are wrong.
    e.   You find yourself using the expression 'Yes, but...'
    f.   You find that you are usually in the company of people who share your ideas.

7   Take a piece of paper and write down three or four sentences describing your home as if to someone who has never been there.   *Chunk size*

Now go through your sentences and count up how many descriptive words you used that were:

    a.   abstract, global descriptions, e.g. spacious, airy, dark, traditional. These are words that are non-specific.
        Number of abstract words =
    b.   detailed, precise descriptions, e.g. $n \times n$ metres, temperature, number of doors, windows etc., colour of the surroundings.
        Number of precise words =

8   Tick any of the following that are characteristic of you   *Personal characteristics*

    a.   Thinking about holidays you have had.
    b.   Savouring the things you see, hear and feel around you now.
    c.   Reviewing how successful your work has been.
    d.   Planning what you will do in the future.
    e.   Paying attention to what is happening around you.
    f.   Mulling over conversations you have had.
    g.   Deciding how you will spend your day.
    h.   Enjoying every moment.
    i.   Dreaming of where you would like to be.
    j.   Being aware of how you feel.
    k.   Anticipating what is going to happen.
    l.   Reminiscing.

Meal

9   Think of the best meal you have ever had. What are you thinking about?

    a.   What happened.
    b.   Who you were with.
    c.   Objects associated with the meal, e.g the food, a present you were given.
    d.   The place — the restaurant, the town, the country or even the location.
    e.   The date, time or the occasion.

Time usage

10   Think of how you most like to spend your time. Which of the following do you think about?

    a.   Being with particular people.
    b.   What you would be doing.
    c.   What you are involved with, e.g. golf clubs, a book, the garden.
    d.   Where you would be.
    e.   A particular time, e.g. a Sunday afternoon, Christmas, the summer.

Future

11   Think of something important that is going to happen in the future. Tick the ones that were a part of your thinking.

    a.   The date, time or occasion.
    b.   What will be happening.
    c.   The people involved.
    d.   The things associated with the future.
    e.   The place.

Success

12   How do you know when you've done a good job? Tick the ones that are true for you.

    a.   Someone praises me.
    b.   I see people using the results of what I have produced.
    c.   I feel good inside.
    d.   **I know I've met the standards I set myself.**
    e.   I get results from the success.
    f.   I congratulate myself.

13 How do you know when you are enjoying yourself?   *Enjoyment*

    a. People around me are happy.
    b. I feel happy with myself.
    c. I have space and time for myself.
    d. Other people are pleased with what is happening.
    e. I appreciate the effect I am having on events around me.
    f. I have a good feeling.

14 What would have to be true for you to be convinced of a new   *Convincer pattern*
    idea or approach? Tick the ones that are true for you.

    a. I'd need to see the idea working.
    b. Someone would have to explain it to me.
    c. I'd need to try it out to know that it worked.
    d. I'd need to see the idea mapped out in some way.
    e. I'd want to discuss it thoroughly.
    f. I'd like some practical experimentation.
    g. I'd need time to think it through.
    h. I'd need to have the idea explained or presented to me a
        number of different times.
    i. I'd like the details.

CHECK YOUR ANSWERS

In this analysis the question numbers are grouped under the particular
filters to which they most relate. For example, questions 1, 2 and 3 are
testing for towards/away from thinking. For explanation of these filters
read Chapter 1.2.

Add up the number of ticks you have in each of these columns: **TOWARDS/AWAY FROM**

	Away from	Towards
Question 1	b	a
	d	c
	f	e
Question 2	b	a
	d	c
	e	f
Question 3	a	b
	f	c
	e	d

The column with the greatest number of ticks indicates your likely
preference.

MATCH/MISMATCH

In question 4 your preference for match or mismatch will be indicated by whether you identified what was similar in each of the shapes.

a.   They are all rectangles, they each have four corners, they all have straight sides.
b.   They are all circles.
c.   They are all arrows, they all point roughly upwards.

The above are all examples of sorting for a match.

If you identified what was different in each, i.e the mismatch, then you would have answers similar to the following:

a.   Two are upright, one is on its side.
b.   Two circles are smaller in size to the other four.
c.   Two arrows are pointing up and right, one is pointing up and left.

For questions 5 and 6, add up the number of ticks in each of the following columns.

	Match	Mismatch
Question 5	a	b
	d	d
	e	f
Question 6	b	a
	c	d
	f	e

The column with the greatest number of ticks indicates your likely preference.

**BIG CHUNK/
SMALL CHUNK**

In question 7, your preference will be indicated by the number of words of each type.

If you have a larger total for (a) your preference is big chunk thinking. A larger total for (b) would indicate a preference for small chunk thinking.

PAST/PRESENT/FUTURE

For question 8, indicate which ones you ticked in the following columns:

Past	Present	Future
a	b	d
c	e	g
f	h	i
l	j	k

The numbers ticked in each column indicate your relative preferences, i.e. highest score = most preferred style; lowest score = least preferred style.

Indicate which ones you ticked in the columns below.

	Activity	Person	Object	Place	Time
Question 9	a	b	c	d	e
Question 10	b	a	c	d	e
Question 11	b	c	d	e	a

Your relative preferences are indicated by the number of ticks in each column, i.e. the more ticks the greater the preference.

	Internal	External
Question 12	c	a
	d	b
	f	e
Question 13	b	a
	c	d
	f	e

Your relative preferences are indicated by the number of ticks in each column, i.e. the more ticks the greater the preference.

The answers you ticked in question 14 would indicate that the following elements would need to be true for you to be convinced of something:

- a. Visual demonstration.
- b. Auditory explanation.
- c. Active experimentation (feelings).
- d. Visual presentation.
- e. Auditory discussion.
- f. Active experimentation (feelings).
- g. Time.
- h. A number of explanations/presentations/ practicals.
- i. Details.

3.4 Write Your Own Metaphor

Aim: To enable you to write a change-inducing story metaphor.
Reference Chapters: 1.3 Enriched Communication; 1.4 Precision Questions; 1.5 Metaphor

1. **Decide on the outcome that you want the metaphor to achieve.** This outcome needs to be one that is in line with the needs and desires of your listener or reader. The unconscious mind is 'pretty smart'. If the metaphor does not fit with the outcomes of your listener or reader their unconscious mind will reject it. Whatever outcome you choose, be aware that the outcome that your reader or listener takes from the metaphor may be entirely different. There are no right or wrong meanings to metaphors. No matter how much people might ask you to tell them the 'meaning', remember that you would only be telling them the meaning as it makes sense to you. By leaving it to their imagination you are encouraging them to make sense of it in their own way.

2. **Choose the style of the metaphor.** The more removed from the issue the metaphor is intended to address, the better. Too much resemblance to reality can provoke resistance in the recipient's mind. However, it helps to choose a theme that does have a place in their mind; something that appeals to their criteria. Choose something that appeals to you too!

3. **Decide on the elements.** For every element of the real life situation choose a parallel element in the metaphor. Think about the connections between these elements and how you can make the connections in the metaphor.

4. **Decide on the twist in the tail.** Introducing a twist or an element of suspense or surprise will engage your listener's attention even more. If the story builds to an unexpected ending it will leave your listeners in a mild form of trance in which their unconscious mind is open to new and creative possibilities.

5. **Use abstract language.** It is important to use abstractions, for example communication, relationship, thought, speech, etc. Use vague nouns such as they, it, a place, people, and vague verbs such as they travelled, journeyed, realised, developed. By keeping the language abstract and ambiguous it allows the mind of your listener to find a meaning that fits for them. This avoids the possibility of resistance from the conscious mind. Keep the timings non-specific, 'Once upon a time, many years ago'.

6. **Use hidden commands.** Put the commands you want your listener to hear into the speech of someone in the story, for example 'the father replied,"Now you too *become a magician*."'

7. **Embellish the telling.** Use enriched language, language that appeals to all the senses. Use gestures, act the story out. Vary your voice tone to add emphasis and drama. Revel in the telling. Improvise the details to suit your listener and incorporate any 'in' jokes that you share with them.

8. **Leave it to their unconscious mind to find its own time to work it out.** You may not be able to tell a story at bedtime to your team or to your customers, but you can choose an occasion when they have time to mull it over.

Model a Skill   3.5

Aim: To enable you to use the skills of NLP to elicit and reproduce a specific skill.
Reference Chapters: 1.6 Modelling specifically although all others are relevant.

1. Identify the skill that you want to model and reproduce. Be specific in the definition of that skill. For example, you may know someone who can:

   - get and hold their audience's attention within seconds of the start of a presentation;
   - make decisions;
   - wake themselves up in the morning without the aid of an alarm clock;
   - set realistic time targets that they consistently achieve.

   Decide specifically what skill you want to reproduce and in what context you want to be able to use it.

2. Select a person, or people, in the company who you consider demonstrate excellence in this skill. Choose the top performers. Be sure you understand what you mean by excellence. Define excellence in terms of the results that your model of excellence achieves. Define excellence in terms of what you see, hear and feel when this top performer is displaying this skill.

3. Observe your model in action to identify the following.

- What specifically they do and how they do it.
- Any subtle behaviour patterns: watch their eye movements and their non-verbal behaviour.
- Their language patterns: which filters do they use?
- What beliefs and values they demonstrate and express.

4. Question your model. First ensure they associate into an experience when they are using the skill you wish to model. When you are certain they are associated (they are imagining themselves using the skill), be sure to keep your questions in the present tense to keep them associated, e.g. 'What are you seeing?', 'What are you saying to yourself?', etc.

   Check out their thinking at each of the logical levels.
   For example:

- 'What are you aware of in your environment?'
- 'What are you saying and doing?' (useful to compare with what they actually said and did in your observations).
- 'What are you thinking?' (watch their eye movements, these will give you more information about their internal strategy than their conscious answer to the question). If you notice them using visual eye accessing cues, for example, ask them, 'What do you see?'
- 'What are your capabilities?'; one of them will be the skill you are modelling.
- 'What is important to you at this time?' (to elicit values).
- 'What do you believe?'— about yourself, about others, about the situation.
- 'How would you describe yourself?' (what is your identity?)
- 'How do you connect with other systems of which you are a part?'

Ensure that you use your NLP core skills, the rapport building especially, as you go through this process.

5. Have someone else model the skill and compare your findings with theirs.

6. Now reproduce the thinking and behaviour patterns of your subject so that you take on their strategy.

7. Test your model by taking away one element at a time as you use it. If the element isn't key to the process it won't make any difference. In some cases taking away an element may even enhance the process.

8. Note the elements and sequence of the final model.

3.6 Take on a Belief of Excellence to Give Yourself New Choices

Aim: To enable you to 'step into' a chosen 'belief of excellence'.

Reference Chapters: 1.2 Filters on your World; 2.1 Write Your Own Lifescript; 2.5 Tap into the Resources You Want

Consider this list and mark yourself against each one.

	I hold this as a belief already	I would like to hold this as a belief
1. Each person is unique.		
2. Everyone makes the best choice available to them at the time.		
3. There is no failure, only feedback.		
4. Behind every behaviour is a positive intention.		
5. The meaning of the communication is its effect.		

	I hold this as a belief already	I would like to hold this as a belief
6. There is a solution to every problem.		
7. The person with the most flexibility in thinking and behaviour has the best chance of succeeding.		
8. Mind and body are part of the same system.		
9. Knowledge, thought, memory and imagination are the result of sequences and combinations of filtering and storing information.		

1. Think of a situation (A) where you would like more choices and where you believe that taking on one of these beliefs of excellence would make the difference that you want. Choose one of the beliefs that you have marked in the 'like to hold' column which you would like to hold in this situation.

2. Identify another situation (B) when this belief must have been true for you no matter how fleeting it may have been.

3. Associate into this time and anchor the feeling of holding this belief with a specific touch.

4. Repeat this process until you experience what it is like to hold this belief each time you fire the anchor.

5. Now as you hold this belief and ensure you continue to hold it, re-experience situation (A) and answer the following questions.
   a. Where are you? What do you see and hear around you?
   b. How do you experience your environment now with this new belief?
   c. In this environment, with this belief, what are you saying and doing?
   d. As you become aware of how you are behaving, what is now possible? What skills do you now have?
   e. With these new skills, what is important to you now?

f.   With this new belief and your awareness of your
     environment, your behaviour, skills and knowing what is
     important to you, what kind of person are you?
g.   How do you connect with all the bigger systems of which
     you are a part — your family, friends, team, company and
     other companies and networks?
h.   What are the benefits to you of holding this belief?
Stay associated into the experience throughout.
You can reinforce the process by imagining each step of the
process marked out spatially on the floor in front of you. The
steps correspond to the logical levels of change (Chapter 2.5).

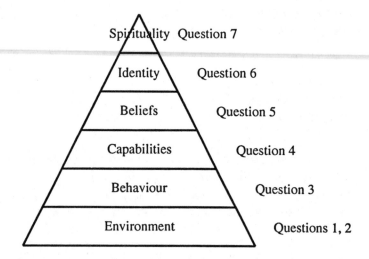

6.   What are your feelings now about presupposing this belief as
     you just did in the exercise? Does it seem desirable? If so,
     write down two situations that are likely to occur in the next
     week where holding this belief would be useful to you.

     Situation 1

     Situation 2

7. Repeat the process from Step 1 through to Step 7 for each of these future situations. Decide how you will remind yourself to presuppose this belief for each of the situations. When the situations have occurred, review how holding this belief affected your experience. Did it work for you? Would you choose to presuppose the belief again in other situations? Generally? How will you do this?

3.7 A Customer Care Checklist

Aim: To review the extent to which you match up to models of excellence in customer care.

Reference Chapters: The relevant chapters are noted against each item on the checklist.

1. Do you have a well formed outcome for your business that is compelling, not only for you but especially for your customers?

   (2.2 Create a Compelling Vision)

2. Do you have a set of beliefs that support your outcome? Do you believe that your customer is at the heart of everything you do? Do all staff understand and live with these beliefs?

   (2.1 Write Your Own Lifescript)

3. Are you able to put yourself into your customer's shoes, to understand their feelings, wants and needs?

   (2.4 Put Yourself in my Shoes)

4. Do you find out your customer's spoken and unspoken requirements?

   (1.4 Precision Questions)

5. Are your customer satisfaction measures expressed in towards or away from terms, i.e. are you measuring what you do want or what you don't want?

   (2.2 Create a Compelling Vision)

6. Do you listen for overt and covert values?

   (2.3 *Develop a Climate of Trust*)

7. Do you build deep levels of rapport with your customer?

   (2.3 *Develop a Climate of Trust*)

Note: This can act as a checklist for the development of your customer care strategy and training for the future.

3.8 Identify Your Learning Strategy

Aim: A company that is continuously improving can only exist if the individuals within it are learning and developing as they work, if they are constantly able to think of and implement new and smarter ways of doing what they do. The ideas you generate count, but more important than that is your ability to manage the way you generate those ideas. This exercise is designed to enable you to increase your awareness of your learning strategy. This in turn will enable you to keep and build on the elements that work well for you and modify any parts that hinder your learning process.

Reference Chapter: 1.1 Thinking Patterns

Steps to identifying your learning strategy

1. Write down a list of as many things as you can think of that you have learned in your lifetime. These can be things that you do or know now that you once had to learn.

2. Select three things from this list as you consider to be examples of effective learning for you.

3. Write out the steps in the learning process for each thing you have selected. Identify what starts the learning process for you, the precise trigger that starts you learning something. Is it, for example, seeing someone doing something especially well? Is it a feeling of inadequacy that you haven't done something as well as you might have done? Is it finding yourself in a new situation that requires you to do something that you have never done before?

4. What happens next and what is the sequence of stages in your learning process?

5. The next part is the fun part. Have you ever seen the way
    advertising agencies lay out their ideas for a new advert
    before committing it to film? They often lay them out in the
    form of a storyboard, rather like a comic strip. Each box
    corresponds to a step in the process.

    Express the common elements of your three most effective
    learning strategies in the form of a storyboard of between five
    and nine pictures. The content of each box can be
    metaphorical. Draw it in a way that signifies the essence of
    that stage in the process. What blocks or hiccups occur along
    the way? What are the closing stages? How do you know when
    you have learned what you set out to learn?

    Here is an example:

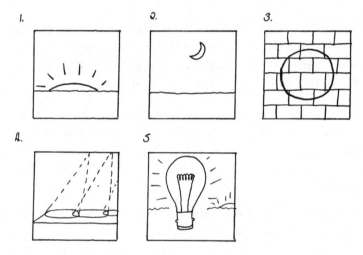

    This was the storyboard for James, a delegate on one of our
    courses.

    Now go through each step of your own storyboard and identify
    the following things:

6. Which thinking and language patterns are dominant in each
    stage, visual/auditory/feelings?

7. Which presupposition is true for each step to occur? For
    example, the trigger that starts the learning process for you —
    is it something you see, is it auditory or do feelings dominate?
    For example, you may go through a stage when you believe
    that you can achieve anything. The presupposition here would
    be that you have all the resources you need to achieve what
    you want.

Here is our example expanded in this way.

'I want to learn something new' (an example of outcome thinking, although not specific), 'It doesn't seem that difficult' (the presupposition being that 'I have all the resources I need to achieve what I want')

'It's much more difficult than I thought' (this has now become problem thinking represented visually by a night sky as opposed to the previous sun rising)

'Now I understand just one part of what I'm trying to learn and I know this bit really well' (rather than thinking globally our course delegate has 'chunked down' in his thinking to focus visually on a small part of the whole. The presupposition now in operation could be that 'there is a solution to every problem')

I now understand several parts and they start to overlap. I start to gain an insight into the whole picture' (visual again, beginning to chunk up to the bigger picture – probably reviving the presupposition that 'I have all the resources I need to achieve what I want')

'I finally have a wide feel for the subject. It all fits together. There are no shadows. In the distance there is more to learn' (now feelings have entered into the thinking as well as the visual elements. It's possible that the presupposition is now that 'there is no failure, only feedback', i.e. there is more to learn)

Once you have this you have the structure of your learning process. You have choice about when and how to apply it.

The result of the subject of our case study working through his strategy for learning in this way was that he recognised how he could apply it to learning French, which he had been trying to do for several years. He had tried listening to tapes in the car and had taken holidays in France where he took opportunities to practise speaking. Although these approaches obviously do work for many people, they hadn't worked for him. He could 'get by' with his French but he didn't have the command of language and the range of vocabulary that he really wanted.

He realised that he learned best by reading and by learning 'one chunk' at a time. He applied this realisation by reading French newspapers and magazines. He concentrated on the written word and put aside any attempt to speak the language. Whenever he could not understand a word he looked it up in a French dictionary (with French definitions). His vocabulary increased dramatically. After a while he began to notice how well he could understand spoken French. His next step will be to speak it effortlessly.

3.9 Prioritise Your Goals as Well Formed Outcomes

Aim: To enable you to select your high priority goals and maximise your chances of achieving them by turning them into well formed outcomes.
Reference Chapters: 1.2 Filters on your World; 2.2 Create a Compelling Vision

1. List all the things you want to achieve for yourself.

	A in 3 mths	B in 6 mths	C in 1 yr	D in 3 yrs	E beyond
Personal (non-work)					
Work related					

2. In each column A, B, C, D and E prioritise the goals you have written down. Put a number 1–5 beside each one in each column (1 = top priority).

3. Now prioritise all the priority 1s (if you have more than one) and for the top three work through each of the elements of a well formed outcome. You will probably find that many of the other outcomes become steps along the way to achieving these. If not, when you are making progress towards or have achieved these three start on the next highest priority three.

4. For /each of your top three goals, work through the following conditions.
   a. Write down in the space overleaf what you *really* want.

Express it in the positive, i.e. what you *do* want not what
you *don't*.

b. Imagine what it will be like to achieve this outcome.
   ● what does it look like?
   ● what does it sound like?
   ● what does it feel like?

c. Decide the context in which you want this outcome.
   Where, when and with whom?

d. Check that it is self-maintained, that the achievement of the
   outcome is down to you alone. It should express the kind of
   person you want to become. If it doesn't, decide what part of
   it is self-maintained and go through steps *a–c* again.
e. Decide if it is worth what it will take to get it. If not, let go
   of the outcome and put your energy into something else
   — choose another goal and start again at *a*. If you believe
   it is worth what it will take, move on to the next step.
f. Identify what your present state does for you.

   What alternative ways are there to satisfy this need that will
   allow you to move towards your outcome?

g. How does having this outcome fit with who you are and
   who you want to become?

h. How does having this outcome fit with other people who
   are important to you in your life?

i. What action steps will you now take to achieve this outcome?

3.10 Identify Your Stoppers to Change

Aim: To enable you to achieve the outcomes you want by working with ways to stop yourself from changing.

Reference Chapter: 2.2 Create a Compelling Vision

1. Make a list of the changes you would like for yourself. List them. These may be the skills you want, a particular lifestyle, material possessions, different relationships, better use of your time.

2. Choose one of these and write down how you stop yourself from achieving it. Examples of stoppers include:
   - Procrastination.
   - Intellectualising about what you want rather than just getting on with it.
   - Seeking out others who will support you in not getting what you want.
   - Imagining the difficulties ahead if you do set out to do what you want. Viewed from the present, difficulties ahead can seem insurmountable and therefore not worth the effort.
   - Finding distractions, other things to do, to worry about, that will delay you starting down the path to change.

● Convincing yourself that change will mean a loss of identity for you, that you will no longer be the person you are today if you change in any way, that you cannot possibly hold on to what you have now as well as having new choices.

3. Identify which of these is the real stopper to achieving what you want. Identify this by applying the following test:

   If this (the stopper) weren't true, would you then be able to achieve your outcomes?

   If the answer is 'no', then this isn't the real stopper to change. If the answer is a congruent 'yes', then this is the real stopper.

4. Turn that stopper into an outcome by asking the question:

   'What do I want instead of this?'

5. Develop this new want into a well formed outcome.
   a. What you really want.

   b. Imagine what it will be like to achieve this outcome:
   ● What does it look like?
   ● What does it sound like?
   ● What does it feel like?

   c. Decide the context in which you want this outcome.

   d. Check that it is self-maintained, that the achievement of the outcome is down to you alone. It should express the kind of person you want to become. If it doesn't, go through steps a–c again, first deciding which part of it is self-maintained.
   e. Decide if it is worth what it will take to get it. If not, let go of the outcome and put your energy into something else — choose another goal and start again at *a*. If you believe it is, move on to the next step.

f.   Identify what your present state does for you.
     What alternative ways are there for you to satisfy this need
     that will allow you to move forward towards your
     outcome?

g.   How does having this outcome fit with who you
     are and who you want to become?

h.   How does having this outcome fit with other
     people who are important in your life?

i.   What action steps will you now take to achieve
     this outcome?

Express Your True Image   3.11

Aims: Image is a state of mind that leaks out of you in everything you say and do. By identifying and associating into your core values you signal to the world your true identity. This exercise will help you to express your core values congruently and communicate your true image.

Reference Chapter: 1.1 Thinking Patterns

You can identify your core values by using Chapter 3.10 or by completing the chart overleaf.

Business

Relationships

Family

Home

Leisure

Health

Fitness

Social

Self-development

1. Using the chart overleaf, write down what is important to you about each of these areas of your life. Add any areas that aren't covered by this list. The things that you write down don't have to be things you have currently, in fact you may be very aware of the fact that you don't have them, but they are things that are important to you. For example, a list might include things like trust, fun, security, a sense of well-being. It is important that you identify the ones that are key for you.

2. Having done this, pick out the ones that are common for you across all the areas of your life.

3. Take three of these core values. Let's suppose they are trust, fun and security. Taking the first one, imagine or remember a time when you had this value in what you were doing or feeling. So, for example, if you have chosen the value of trust choose a time when you experienced trust in exactly the way that is important to you.

    You can do this exercise sitting or standing. It helps to mark out a different physical place for each of the values. If you do the exercise with the help of someone else, ask them to give you feedback subsequently on how your external image changed as you went through each phase.

4. Choose a place where you will step into your experience of having the first core value you have identified. As you remember the time of this experience and as the memory of it builds, step into the place you have mentally marked out as representing this value. Step in by fully associating into that experience as if you are there again. You will be seeing it through your own eyes, hearing it through your own ears and reliving the feelings you had then.

5. Once you have fully associated into core value 1, keep hold of that feeling as you begin to think of a time when you experienced core value 2 (in our example, fun). As your memory of that time grows, step into the place you have marked out as representing this second core value, taking with you the experience of core value 1. Fully associate into this experience.

6. Repeat this process for core value 3 so that you have the experience and the feelings of associating into each of your core values simultaneously.

7. Break state.

8. Repeat the process several times until you can automatically access the experience and the resources associated with each of your core values.

The more you do this the more you will begin to express and live these values. The interesting thing about image is that once you become and live out your values, you start to attract people and situations that fit these same values.

Establish Your Core Values 3.12

Aim: The values you hold will have an order of priority for you. Some override others. This exercise is designed to enable you to identify the high priority, *core* values, the ones that are at the heart of everything you say and do.

Reference Chapter: 2.2 Create a Compelling Vision

1. Think of something typical of you that you choose to do regularly. It may be a hobby or interest that you have or work that you choose to do.

2. Write it here.

   A

   _____

   What would have to be true to *just* tip the balance for you to decide not to do A?

   B

   _____

Assuming that B is true, what would also have to be true to *just* tip the balance for you to decide to do A?

C

_____

Assuming that B and C are both true, what would have to be true to *just* tip the balance for you to decide not to do A?

D

_____

You can continue up this chain using the alternating questions, each time taking all of the previous conditions to be true. In doing so you are establishing your hierarchy of values. Each time you establish a new factor to tip the balance one way or the other, you are identifying a higher level value, one that overrides the ones that have gone before.

Eventually you will reach your core values, the ones that are at the top of the hierarchy for you. A successful outcome to a negotiation will meet the core values of all the parties involved.

Experience the Different Perceptual Positions

3.13

Aim: To enable you to develop your ability to experience 1st, 2nd and 3rd position and thereby create understanding and choice in a situation that may have become blocked.

Reference Chapter: 2.4 Put Yourself in my Shoes

HOW TO EXPERIENCE 1ST POSITION

Find yourself a quiet, comfortable place. Organise the lighting so that it is not too bright, not too dim. Ensure there are no time pressures on you.

Pay attention to your surroundings, what you can see around you. Notice the shapes and forms. See how the shapes cast shadows. What colour and shades do you see?

Attend to what you can hear, what sounds there are, how loud, what frequency. Take your time. Now turn your attention to yourself. What parts of your body can you see, what movement is there? What sounds can you hear that you are making?

What can you feel? The pressure of your feet on the floor? The weight of your body on the chair/bed? Which parts are touching, where is the greatest, least pressure? Where are your hands and arms resting? Where can you feel them touch? Is your head resting on anything? What is taking the weight of your head? What can you smell? What taste is in your mouth?

What internal emotions do you feel? What intensity do these feelings have? What is their location? What are the characteristics of the feelings?

This awareness of yourself in this way is 1st position thinking.

How familiar is this for you? If it is familiar to experience the world in this way then 1st position is a way of thinking and experiencing situations that probably comes naturally to you.

Ask a friend to participate in this exercise with you. It will take at least 15 minutes and can be conducted anywhere, inside or outside.

HOW TO EXPERIENCE 2ND POSITION

It is based on an ancient Indian ritual, 'walking in someone else's moccasins'. You are both going to go for a walk but you will follow in your friend's footsteps approximately 2 metres behind.

As you walk get into the rhythm of your friend's walk, take their strides, go at their pace. Pay attention to where they look, look at the same things, hold your head in the same way. It will be as if you are their shadow.

Do this without speaking.

When 15 minutes are up tell your friend what your experience of the walk was, what you were thinking and feeling. Compare your experience to their experience of the walk. You may be surprised at how close your experiences can be. This is 2nd position behaviour and thinking.

You don't need to go for a walk every time you want to experience 2nd position. However, adopting the posture and movement of the other person is a way of stepping into their experience of the world.

The other person need not be present. Create an image in your mind of the behaviour and posture of the other person. What do they say and how do they say it? What has to be true for them to behave and speak as they do? What is their identity, what are their beliefs and values? What skills and qualities are they bringing to bear on the situation? What are they experiencing around them?

AN ALTERNATIVE WAY OF EXPERIENCING 2ND POSITION

Now step into their shoes. Match their behaviour. Take on their identity, beliefs, values, capabilities and experience. What is the world like through their eyes and ears? What do you feel in this position? When you have fully stepped into 2nd position, the reactions and feelings of this other person will make sense, they will seem normal, a natural way to behave.

Think of a situation that involved you and one other person. Recall where this situation took place, what was said and how you were feeling.

HOW TO EXPERIENCE 3RD POSITION

A genuine 3rd position comes from having experienced a situation in 1st and 2nd positions first (hence the numbers!).

So experience the situation from 1st person, allowing yourself to be in your own shoes, seeing, hearing and feeling the situation from within your own body.

When you have fully experienced 1st position, step into 2nd position. You may find that moving position helps you to break out of 1st position and cleanly enter into 2nd. In 2nd allow yourself to experience the situation as if in the other person's shoes. Use the steps outlined in (3) to do this.

Having experienced 2nd position, step out so that you can see and hear yourself and the other person as if you are an observer. Ensure that the 'you' in the situation and the other person are equidistant from you and at eye level. Hear the 'you' in the situation and the other person.

If you are experiencing any emotions, then imagine switching these emotions into the person to whom they belong, i.e. the 'you' in the situation or the other person.

This ability to detach yourself in your thinking is the ability to take 3rd position.

NOTES

It takes skill and practice to be able to experience each of the positions fully. It usually helps to have someone else with you as you practise moving through the positions, as it can be easy to delude yourself that you are in a position when in fact you are not.

For example, you might believe that you are in 1st position when in fact you might be carrying some of the feelings that belong to the other person. Similarly, you might think you are in 2nd position when you are only intellectualising about what it would be like to be in the other person's shoes. And you might think you are taking the detached 3rd position when an observer might be able to detect that you are slipping into 1st or 2nd again.

Learning to recognise the characteristics of the pure states will help you to use each of the positions cleanly and skilfully and increasingly achieve win/win outcomes in all areas of your life.

Use Perceptual Positions to Become More Assertive

3.14

Aim: Assertion is about balance, balance in your ability to consider your needs and wants with those of others. The way you think about your past, present and future situations affects that balance. This exercise will help you to think about your experiences in a way that enables you to align yourself in the way you speak and act.

Reference Chapters: 1.1 Thinking Patterns; 2.4 Put Yourself in my Shoes

1. Think of a current or future situation — one that you would like to be able to handle assertively. It may be characteristic of situations that you have handled aggressively or non-assertively in the past. Imagine yourself in this situation and pay attention to how you see, hear and feel this situation.

2. Step into 1st position so that you are seeing, hearing and feeling the situation as if you are in your own shoes. Experiment with your thinking patterns and the distinctions in these thinking patterns until you have a balanced representation in your thinking, i.e. you are on the same eye level as the other person, you are both speaking with equal volume and the feelings you are experiencing are your own feelings. If not, give them back to the rightful owner. Imagine yourself doing that. Break state.

3. Step into the shoes of the other person (2nd position) and go through the same process to bring balance into your thinking if it is not already there. Check out the visual, the auditory and the feeling elements. Break state.

4. Stand back and move into 3rd position. Ensure that you are equidistant and at the same height as the 'you' in the picture and the other person. Balance the sounds and the voices you hear so that they too are equal in volume and quality. Finally, check out the feelings. Are there any? If so give them to the owner, the 'you' in the picture, or the other person or anyone else to whom they belong. Being in this 3rd position means standing back from emotion in order to consider the situation objectively and dispassionately. Break state.

5. Step again into 1st position, having balanced your thinking in each position, and pay attention to how you now experience this situation. If you have succeeded in bringing a balance you should now have new understanding and new choices about to proceed in a way that is likely to meet the needs of all parties involved.

Appendix 1
Answers to Thought Provokers

Some of the thought provokers were designed to do just that —
provoke thought — and as such, have no answers. Those questions are
therefore not included in this answer set.

1.1 Thinking Patterns

1a. People whose preference is visual do well in jobs that involve
dealing with design, layout, colour, images, for example:

- artistic design

- advertising

- image design

- photography

- interior design

1b. People whose preference is auditory enjoy work that involves
the use of words, discussion and sound, for example:

- publishing

- sound recording

- musician

- telephone — sales/reception/customer handling

1c. People with a feelings preference would fit with jobs that involve them using their instinct, with work that involves using their sense of touch and, depending on their specific preference, work that draws on their sense of taste or smell. For example:

- counselling

- carpentry

- sculpture

- cookery

Generally, it is an advantage to be able to use all of your senses — rarely does a job involve you using one skill exclusively. However, by recognising your preferences it helps to ensure that the main elements of the work utilise the strengths you have.

2. The way you represent the outcome of the meeting indicates your likely preference for visual/auditory/feelings. It may be a combination of any or all systems.

3. Watching eye movements helps you to begin to understand how other people might be processing information. Remember that some people's eye movements are reversed, i.e. up and to their right might for them indicate that they are remembering an image. Keep an open mind — observe and listen for their patterns.

4. and 5.   Identifying distinctions in the way you think about something can help you to develop your awareness of how the way you think affects your attitude and experience. It is not the content that matters here, it is the quality of visual, auditory and feelings distinctions that affect your response.

1.2 Filters on your world

1. The author of this passage sorts primarily for activity. They refer predominantly to what they do.

2. This person suggests that they mismatch and operate at a small chunk level.

3. This person has an 'away from' filter and also sorts primarily for people.

1.3 Enriched Communication

1. You could prepare to present some of your ideas visually, e.g. by drawing them on a flipchart or notepad. You could plan how you might discuss the ideas. You could involve them if possible by giving a practical demonstration in which they could use the ideas you are promoting. Throughout your meeting you would use visual/auditory and feelings language.

2. Examples of possible answers that use enriched language:
   a. I'd really like to be seen to be progressing within this organisation. I'd like to be able to say to myself, 'I've made significant progress' and then I'd feel very satisfied.
   b. Let me explain what I want to achieve in this meeting. I'd like to get clear first what we all want so that we feel confident what we are here for.

4. Some suggestions are:
   a. *Visual*: By using diagrams and pictures on the overhead projector, slide projector or flipchart. You can use visual language to paint pictures with words. By making the environment attractive.
   b. *Auditory*: By explaining your ideas and allowing discussion and questions. By adding variety in your voice and by using auditory language. By paying attention to sounds, e.g. having music in the background as people arrive.
   c. Feelings: By allowing 'hands on' if it is a demonstration. By giving your audience something to touch and hold. By appealing to their emotions and by using feelings language. By making the environment appealing to their sense of touch, taste and smell, e.g. ensuring that it is comfortable, that there is something to drink and that it smells good — maybe some fragrant fresh flowers.

1.4 Precision Questions

4. Some suggestions:
   a. What would happen if you did?
   b. No one? How would you want someone to help you?
   c. How do you know that? Who are you referring to?
   d. Who did what deliberately and how do you know that?
   e. How does me being late make you annoyed?

    f.   According to whom?

    g.   How do you direct them and how would you like them to respond?

    h.   According to whom? Who is or isn't relating to whom and in what way?

    i.   How are you getting yourself upset?

    j.   How did I upset you?

2.2 Create a Compelling Vision

1.   A lot depends on how these are said, as the words might convey either pattern but the way in which they are said communicates something else. However, taking the words alone:

    a.   Towards (although the words alone have a 'longing for' quality characteristic of 'away from' thinking).

    b.   Away from.

    c.   Towards.

2.   When someone says they will 'try' to do something for you it usually carries with it the implication that they don't expect to succeed. Even if they 'try hard' it may mean that they put a lot of effort in but ultimately deny themselves success.

2.4 Put Yourself in my Shoes

1.   The answers below are meant as examples. The only right answer for a positive intention is the one that makes sense of all the behaviour for you. When you find a positive intention that explains all the behaviours you will feel completely different about the behaviour towards you in a way that gives you understanding and choice.

    However, examples of positive intentions are:

    a.   For you to learn how to demonstrate commitment or for you to learn influencing skills that will change your manager's mind. It could be that your manager's positive intention towards you is for you to be sure about what you really want.

    b.   For you to learn how to communicate in a compelling way or for you to know when your communication is not interesting so that you will recognise this when it happens at other times and with other people

    c. For you to learn how to manage change. For you to
        know where your time commitment lies.

    d. For you to re-evaluate what you really want. To test
        your resolve in going for what you want. For you to learn how
        to handle rejection constructively.

    e. For you to learn how to build rapport so that you
        can influence people outside your authority.

2a.   1st position.

2b.   3rd position.

2c.   2nd position.

Appendix 2
Bibliography

Recommended NLP starter books

Connirae Andreas & Steve Andreas, *Heart of the Mind*, Real People Press, 1989.

Steve Andreas and Connirae Andreas, *Change Your Mind and Keep the Change*, Real People Press, 1987.

Genie Z Laborde, *Influencing with Integrity*, Syntony Publishing, 1984.

Genie Z Laborde, *Fine Tune Your Brain*, Syntony Publishing, 1988.

Joseph O'Connor & John Seymour, *Introducing NLP*, Aquarian Press, 1993.

Popularised NLP

Kerry L Johnson, *Selling with NLP*, Nicholas Brealey, 1994.

Anthony Robbins, *Awaken the Giant Within*, Simon & Schuster, 1992.

Denis Waitley, *Seeds of Greatness*, Cedar, 1990.

Further NLP

Connirae Andreas & Tamara Andreas, *Core Transformation*, Real People Press, 1994.

Richard Bandler, *The Adventures of Anybody*, Meta Publications, 1993.

Richard Bandler & John Grinder, *Frogs Into Princes*, Real People Press, 1979.

Leslie Cameron-Bandler, *Solutions*, Future Pace, 1985.

Leslie Cameron-Bandler, David Gordon & Michael Lebeau, *The Emprint Method*, Future Pace, 1985.

Robert Dilts, *Changing Belief Systems with NLP*, Meta Publications, 1990.

Robert Dilts, Tim Hallborn & Suze Smith, *Beliefs*, Metamorphous Press, 1993.

John Grinder & Richard Bandler, *The Structure of Magic, Parts I and II*, Science & Behaviour Books, 1976.

Scout Lee & Jan Summers, *The Challenge of Excellence*, Metamorphous Press, 1990.

Terence L McClendon, *The Wild Days of* NLP 1972–1981, Meta Publications, 1989.

NLP Influences

Gregory Bateson, *Steps to an Ecology of Mind*, Ballantine Books, 1988.

Noam Chomsky, *Aspects of the Theory of Syntax*, MIT Press, 1965.

Alfred Korzybski, *Science and Sanity*, The International Non-Aristotelian Library Publishing Company.

Frederick S Perls, *Gestalt Therapy Verbatim*, Real People Press, 1979.

Virginia Satir, *Peoplemaking*, Science and Behaviour Books, 1989.

Johanna Schwab, *A Resource Handbook for Satir Concepts*, Science & Behaviour Books, 1990.

Paul Watzlawick, *The Language of Change*, W W Norton, 1993.

Paul Watzlawick, John Weakland and Richard Fisch, *Change*, W W Norton & Co, 1974.

The Gestalt Approach: Eyewitness to Therapy, Science and Behaviour Books, 1973.

Business

John Adair, *Not Bosses But Leaders*, Kogan Page, 1990.

Robert E Alberti & Michael L Emmons, *Your Perfect Right*, Impact, 1977.

Ken and Kate Back, *Assertiveness at Work*, McGraw-Hill, 1982.

David Freemantle, *Incredible Bosses*, McGraw-Hill, 1990.

Eliyahu M Goldratt & Jeff Cox, *The Goal: Beating the Competition*, Creative Output Books, 1986.

Eliyahu M Goldratt, *It's Not Luck*, Gower, 1994.

Andrew S Grove, *High Output Management*, Random Grove, 1983.

Charles Handy, *The Empty Raincoat*, Hutchinson, 1994.

John Harvey-Jones, *Making it Happen*, William Collins, 1988.

Alistair Mant, *Leaders We Deserve*, Basil Blackwell, 1985.

Paddy O'Brien, *Positive Management*, Nicholas Brealey, 1992.

Barrie Pearson, *Common-sense Business Strategy*, Mercury Books, 1991.

Tom Peters and Nancy Austin, *A Passion for Excellence*, Fontana, 1986.

Gefford Pinchott III, *Intrapreneuring*, Harper & Row, 1986.

Anita Roddick, *Body and Soul*, Vermillion, 1992.

Sidney B Simon, *In Search of Values*, Warner Books, 1993.

John Whitmore, *Coaching for Performance*, Nicholas Brealey, 1992.

Mike Woodcock and Dave Francis, *Clarifying Organizational Values*, Gower, 1989.

R L Wing, *The Art of Strategy*, The Aquarian Press, 1989.

Other related topics and sources of inspiration

Edward de Bono, *Handbook for the Positive Revolution*, Penguin Books, 1991.

William C Byham with Jeff Cox, *Zapp! The Lightning of Empowerment*, Business Books, 1991.

Gene Early, *Developing Couple Relationships*, S M Olsen, 1988.

Mark Fisher, *The Instant Millionaire*, Hammond, 1993.

Charles Handy, *Waiting for the Mountain to Move*, Arrow, 1992.

John Heider, *The Tao of Leadership*, Wildwood House, 1986.

David Hemery, *Sporting Excellence*, Collins Willow, 1986.

Peter Honey, *Improve Your People Skills*, Institute of Personnel Management, 1988.

M James & D Jongeward, *Born to Win*, Addison Wesley, 1971.

Spencer Johnson, *Yes or No*, Harper Collins, 1992.

Peter Kline, *The Everyday Genius*, Great Ocean Publishers, 1988.

James Morrison & John O'Hearne, *Practical Transactional Analysis in Management*, Addison Wesley, 1977.

Vincent Nolan, *The Innovator's Handbook*, Sphere Books, 1990.

Robert Thomson, *The Psychology of Thinking*, Penguin, 1971.

R L Wing, *The Tao of Power*, Aquarian Press, 1986.

Metaphor

David Gordon, *Therapeutic Metaphors*, Meta Publications, 1978.

John Harricharan, *When You Can Walk on Water, Take the Boat*, Aquarian,

Dan Millman, *The Peaceful Warrior*, H J Kramer, 1984.

Lee Wallas, *Stories for the Third Ear*, Norton, 1985.

Nelson Zink, *The Structure of Delight*, Mind Matters, 1991.